SAVING HUMANITY:

Life Based in Positive Social Values

*Reminders about maintaining the good life
for all of us*

Tom Gnagey

The Family of Man Press

(C) 2021

Why this Book?

My Mother encouraged me to enjoy the moment. Father
urged me to prepare for the future. Grandpa suggested that
however I went about my life, to do it in a decent manner. They
all modeled unconditional love.
Was I the luckiest kid in history or what?

Along the way,
I have acquired additional positive values,
but those four alone have guided me along a path
that set me on course to be one of the good guys in the world,
one who worked to maintain and improve the human condition
and keep things right among men.

I was one of the fortunate ones.
Many have not been.
Mankind either eliminates 'negative values'
like greed, selfishness, power hunger, and vengeance,
or mankind will destroy itself.

Here is what we do!
It is time to stop handwringing over the terrible state of things
and roll up our sleeves and get to work.
This book provides a simple plan to save the human species:
Every day we must demonstrate the danger of
Harmful Social Values,
while we base our lives on
Positive Social Values,
and
Consistently and regularly model them to the children.

– Tom Gnagey

PREFACE

Interestingly, you will find nothing new here; the solution has been with us for centuries. Too many have chosen to ignore it or let it slip. Perhaps the novel approach presented here can help make the difference.

You will immediately determine this book is written following to the 'Spiral of Knowledge' technique – a few bits of information are presented and then those bits are expanded and amplified as are those and those until eventually the information has come together as the complete, integrated message. When you find some piece of information is not immediately clear, don't go away, it will come around again, soon. I hope you find it interesting and helpful.

The names used in this book
have been changed
for reasons of privacy.

SECTION ONE
The Fascinating Basics:
What are values, what do they do, and how do we come by them?

Surely, a species as potentially intelligent as Human Beings should be able to recognize the folly of willingly following blatantly self-destructive paths, yet our history suggests that generation after generation, for thousands of years, we have done just that. It has been a matter of letting positive social values too easily deteriorate into harmful social values. What are values, how are they acquired, and why do they matter – why do they represent the thin edge between the survival and destruction of mankind? It will be these and related concepts we will be exploring and analyzing in the following pages.

For many, this book will be a review of things already understood. For them, I hope it can become a way of organizing, realigning, and more effectively applying what we know in the service of saving humanity from destroying itself.

First, what is a value? A value is a belief or conviction powerful enough to dependably guide one's behavior. If I value *compassion*, I allocate my time and resources and act in ways that are helpful to others and that ease pain and suffering. If I value *stuff*, I allocate my time and resources and act in ways that help me accumulate vast amounts of money, power, and/or material things – a closet full of shoes or jeans rather than regular, meaningful contributions to agencies that make sure no child must go to bed hungry.

What is a POSITIVE SOCIAL VALUE? Positive Social Values are those that protect, maintain, and improve society – love rather than hate, productivity rather than sloth, humor rather than cheerlessness, helpful rather than hurtful or disturbing, peace rather than war or discord or tension.

What about *NEGATIVE SOCIAL VALUES?*

Let me share a bit of background. As a young psychologist, I was called to examine a fourteen-year-old boy who had been keeping his orphanage in an uproar since his arrival two weeks earlier. Among the tests I administered was one to assess his self-esteem – briefly, how well he liked himself. Another had him make choices that indicated what values guided his life. He scored extremely high on the self-esteem test – he really liked himself. On the value test, he scored very low – he chose those that would destroy society (hate not love, hurtful not helpful, and so on). In my naivete, I couldn't understand that: how could a person who described himself as denying positive social values and embracing negative social values, like himself? He was by all definitions – even his own – a 'bad' boy and he liked himself that way. The discovery was helpful – one's level of self-esteem had little to do with how 'good' (life-enhancing) a person he might be.

Most every Positive Social Value has an opposite, destructive, Negative Social Value. Both are acquired in the same way – they reflect the experiences a person has early in life (happily, there can be remediated exceptions to that). When he accepts the values of his 'group' and is praised for it, he develops high self-esteem. In Native American lore, up until a child is four years of age, he listens to what sort of person he is told he is, and he spends the rest of his life proving it. Children who hear they are caring and helpful and abide by the rules, are most likely to grow into caring and helpful adults who abide by the rules. Those who hear they are the 'me first', break the rules they don't like sort, grow up to be just that.

In terms of the premise of this book – saving humanity by demonstrating and instilling Positive Social Values – the people who pose the greatest danger to our species are, like the boy at the orphanage, those that like the fact they live their lives according to negative social values – the Disruptors, the Destroyers, the Hurters, the Hoarders, the Selfish. We will revisit and develop this concept often.

How are values acquired? Children study adults – after all, growing up is their principal goal, so kids understand they have to learn how to be an adult. Recall one of the frequent phrases of childhood: 'When I grow up . . ." They tend to believe what they *see* in adults' behavior more than they believe what adults *say or tell* them. Simply put, values are acquired by paying close attention to the values modeled by the grown-ups with whom they interact. Dad brags about 'pulling the wool over somebody's eyes' and the child learns taking advantage of others is an acceptable way of life. Big brother takes time to help him with his math homework and he learns that helpfulness, kindness, and patience, are ways of life to be valued and practiced. (More, 'how-to-do-its', as we proceed.)

Values of some sort WILL be learned. The reader will see the logic in having parents thoughtfully model what values they want the child to learn rather than just letting a random set fall into place willy-nilly. Parents must decide on a few values they want to be sure their child acquires to get him started on a positive path in the world. (Positive values are like magnets that attract others as life unfolds.) We accomplish that by modeling them regularly and consistently, making sure the children observe the positive outcomes. Talk about the values in tender, loving, respectful ways – wrap them in positive emotions and make the process a big deal so the *Deep Mind* pays attention (much more about the Deep Mind just below. It is virtually always left out of value discussions. Here it will take center stage.).

Why do values matter? Which of these values rather consistently create a positive, helpful, fulfilling way of life – 'taking advantage of others' or 'helpfulness, kindness, and patience' toward others? Which of them lead to a safe and comfortable way of life? Consider another example: Big brother is a brawler, applying his fists first and words (perhaps) later. Big sister is a diplomat, a negotiator, a peacemaker. One sees how little brother's life will follow significantly different paths depending on which of those values he comes to accept – the first personally and socially destructive and the second personally and socially supportive and beneficial.

Values also matter because they become the basis for *Integrity,* and only people of integrity will save humanity. Think of integrity as a foundation of positive values one always lives up to (or according to). A person of integrity doesn't 'slip a value' in order to kowtow to somebody or gain some favor or protect himself from criticism – he knows what he believes, and he sticks with it, regardless. As will become clear from each set of values that will be presented here, a person always has the choice between Door Number One or Door Number Two – the positive one or the harmful one. People without Integrity become undependable, despicable sorts of folks, ones who do not contribute to Humanity's comfort and survival – instead, typically contributing to its downfall or extinction – as a minimum, to its discomfort. [An early 2000s survey out of the University of Maryland, found the professions perceived to have the lowest levels of integrity were politicians and lawyers.]

Initially, values are established as Simple Values – single feature values – love/hate, kind/hurtful. Later in life, Complex Values are assembled. They are a collection of compatible simple values associated with a complex topic – think, 'I value democracy', 'love for my mate or child', 'determination to save the planet'. It will be instructive to select a complex value and determine what simple values make it up. (Perhaps, wait until after the reader has become more specifically reminded of the two dozen Simple Value pairs that are presented below – really, they *are* going to be presented!)

A brief examination of four, *negative* value-based examples will set the stage for what follows.

1) Greed (a negative value) divides us into the *haves* and the *have-nots*, the rich and the impoverished, those who usurp the wealth of society and those who are left helpless and without the basic necessities for a good or even adequate life. Such division in a society leads to suffering and helplessness in an ever-growing portion of the population – *ever-growing* because most Have Nots have no way of turning around their lot in life, while the Powerful Greedy find ways of destroying even the Just Less Powerful Greedy, so wealth becomes consolidated in fewer and fewer hands.

2) Division (the negative opposite of *inclusion*) divides humanity into 'Us' and 'Them' camps. Divisions are made along some trait-based line. Values that separate us establish distance between groups, which leads to less understanding and increased misunderstanding – unless we rub shoulders with somebody, we can't get to know and appreciate them; in fact, we may well fear them or believe they do not wish us well. In one of the little towns where I lived briefly, it was between the town kids and the 'wrong-siders' – the families who lived on the poor side of the tracks. We didn't play together. In many instances that was promoted equally by each group. The groups were to some extent frightened by each other. When I made a 'wrong-sider' my friend, the parents of my best friend forbade him from playing with me anymore. *Knowledge* about, not *ignorance* or inaccurate lore about, another group is what will cool animosities and fears and lead the groups toward understanding and peace rather than division. It requires an ongoing, thoughtful, purposeful, approach.

3) Hate, in its purest state, seeks the annihilation of another person or group of people. It is often used to represent some lesser feeling or desire, but the *preservation* of the hated one is *never* a consideration. Love is often proposed as the opposite. To be accurate, love's typical definition must be extended to include protection and preservation. A parent or spouse or sibling or child understands that love moves well beyond intense fondness, as love is often characterized. Hate degrades or eliminates; Love builds up and preserves. Us and them are all we have. Eliminate *them*, and we lose their considerable pool of skills – we are alone and defenseless. Incorporate *them* and our chances of survival greatly increase, and life grows in positive ways. Hate often partners with Revenge and we will investigate that devastating pair later.

4) Selfishness puts oneself first above others. 'My needs come first regardless of how that may affect anybody else.' It fails to recognize that without others, one could not survive. It fails to recognize that being surrounded by happy, content, well cared for people tends to make one's own life happy, content and safe. Selfishness is a close relative of Greed. *Selfishness* says, 'I want, need, and deserve most everything of value.' *Greed* goes out and gets it. When most of the wealth is held by a small percent of the citizens, both greed and selfishness are sure to be in play. The opposite of Selfishness can be thought of as Self*less*ness – gladly giving of oneself and possessions for the benefit of those who are in need and *that* is a close relative of altruism. Those will be explored just ahead.

It will be our journey here, to examine pairs of Values – a Socially Positive Value with its 'opposite', Socially Harmful Value, and run each of them to their logical conclusions – discover how the world would operate if one or the other value controlled human behavior.

One further characteristic of these pairs: they are *Mutually Incompatible Alternatives*. That is, if one is present the other cannot be present – love/hate, respect/contempt, selfishness/ altruism. The Deep Mind may harbor remnants of both extremes, but the one, which was set there most recently and with the most emotional impact, is the one most likely to be acted upon – that is, most likely to direct one's life. When both are of nearly equal power, mental disturbance is possible if not likely – the old, 'torn between A and B' conundrum. Consider the situation in which the young child sees his dad modeling hate and his mother modeling love – ouch!!!!!

A mini-side trip here. When I lived at home, mother always approached me with the same comment whenever I left for play or school or whatever: *"Remember who you are, Tommy"*. It was the implementation of the point above – frequent 'rehearsal' or resetting of the positive values my family and I shared. The way my parents approached it required *my* active thought – not, hearing 'do this or do that,' – *I* was required to do the remembering of who I was. That suggestion was usually accompanied by an embrace or kiss – strong emotional reinforcement. Mother had never heard of a Deep Mind, but she understood the concept well – frequent rehearsal wrapped in positive emotion. End of side-trip.

I have had seminar participants list over two hundred Pairs of Values, so which did I pick to examine here? I used several criteria: Do they represent common, real-life value choices that come up daily? Do they lend themselves to simple, short, relatable, illustrations? Do they clearly relate to the topic of the book – Saving Humanity? A few others probably slipped in here and there.

Back in my clinical psychologist days, a 65-year-old woman sought my help because of her life-long fear of caterpillars. They terrified her to the point that on some occasions she lost control of her bladder and even fainted at their presence. It seems when she was quite young, her older brother (they are often soooo helpful) convinced her their bite was deadly, and he would chase her with them, terrifying her. As she matured, the conscious part of her mind came to know they were not deadly. The deepest part of her mind that controlled her emotional reactions believed they were real, however, and no amount of 'facts' could change that. I was able to help her remove the hurtful 'directive' that had been well established in her deep mind, and she was able to leave the fear behind her. Please, keep the story in mind.

The Deep Mind is the deepest, most hidden part of the human mind and it ultimately directs our behavior. It is a part we cannot easily access and know about. I have dealt with that in detail in my book, *Deep Mind Mastery** and will only hit the highlights here that have impact on the values we accept, hold, and demonstrate. (Essentially, live and die by.)

The *prime directive* of the Deep Mind is to preserve the life of 'it's person'. Few things can overpower that directive (assuring the safety of family members being one). When it has reason to feel threatened, or even when it just cannot be sure it is in a safe situation, the Deep Mind directs us to proceed with great caution and protect ourselves from the perceived or possible threat. That which is *different* quickly and easily becomes threatening. Therefore, the less experienced and less educated, who have a less complete understanding of the nature of the universe, tend to feel threatened more easily and often, and by more aspects of the world – different people, philosophies, customs – even looks.

If one has never come to know Green People, he will initially feel threatened by, or at least suspicious of, the Green Family that moves in next door. Just in case, he may be moved to protect himself and his loved ones from Green People by avoiding them or isolating the newcomers, or, in the extreme, doing away with them in order to feel safe from whatever malevolence they just might soon direct toward him. Taking time to learn about the Green Ones tends to moderate such irrational fear and apprehension – most new people do not have harmful intentions, but if one is not open to getting to know them, one cannot be sure. In Deep Mind survival thinking, 'If they are not <u>for</u> <u>sure</u> *safe*, treat them as *dangerous*'. (If one hasn't had a variety of interactions – one on one – with black people, white people, Jews or Muslims, Orientals, educated folks, street people, science believers, they will initially be categorized as different, and how is the Deep Mind programed to react to *different* – with caution, suspicion, and fear in the service of one's continued wellbeing.)

Often, instead of making the reasonable effort to learn about another group, the 'elders' find it easier (safer) to concoct frightening stories about that group – an effective way of convincing their 'tribe' to see them as dangerous so they will stay away from them (and never learn the truth about them). It has long been a way for the 'elders' to solidify their influence and power. At age ten, my patient's brother had the mechanics of the process down pat: "You can't learn the truth about a caterpillar if you don't interact *naturally* with caterpillars, and if you're scared of them you won't interact."

A point to ponder: The Deep Mind, essential for our survival, is also the promoter of prejudice and separation (as it acts on its prime directive to protect us), and *that* will destroy us. We must follow a thoughtful, enlightened path to allow two essential functions of the deep mind to work their beneficial strengths for us (inquisitiveness and fear).

Helping youngsters become eager to (safely) learn about that which is new to them, different from them, and that which they do not understand, is, perhaps, *the most basic value along the road to world peace and human survival* (and personal and species-wide growth and development). It has most often been called an 'open approach' compared with a 'closed approach' to human interaction. The concept will be clarified and expanded as the discussion proceeds. For example, why religions virtually universally require the 'closed approach' when it comes to investigating other belief systems. (And why comfortably religious people do the same – don't let new information rock their religious boat – promoting their intentional ignorance.)

The Deep Mind believes whatever it thinks its person has told it, and it is NOT a good or accurate listener because it uses language poorly. (I'm a good guy, I'm a bad guy, Green Guys are dangerous, compassion is good, compassion shows I am weak, I must keep what I have because I might need it someday, and so on).

Visualize it this way: a long row of open, 'mailbox-like' cubbyholes stretching, side by side, in a long row. The contents of the boxes toward the left end are noticed and believed by the Deep Mind most easily and reliably. Those toward the right, less so. Let's say each value is written on an index card and those cards can move from cubby hole to cubby hole depending on the characteristics possessed by each and changes in the person's situation. Values acted upon most frequently, most repetitively, with the most emotion and accompanied by images will congregate on the left end and become easily and immediately available for use. Those that aren't, move to the right. (More to come)

Early in one's life, that 'telling' about a person to its Deep Mind is largely done by the people around it. Gradually, the child grows to be more in control of the messaging (but not dependably so until the brain's logical and judgement abilities solidify in his or her early twenties – a reason that clergymen, cultists, military organizations, and politicians go after still vulnerable teenagers).

Those first four years of life leave an indelible mark on a person's Deep Mind Direction System that becomes reliably hard to shake or modify. Parents and care givers must be thoughtful about what they foist upon defenseless, young, Deep Minds – will those directives be helpful throughout the child's life, do they allow the child to later think for himself in a world the parents can't even envision, do they 'rule by fear?" I will repeat, fear becomes extremely difficult to reduce or eliminate once the Deep Mind takes hold of it. Sometimes, fear has a way of disconnecting from what it was paired with originally (monsters under the bed, caterpillars) and just hangs out as nonspecific fear threatening and agitating the Deep Mind for no apparent reason (free-floating anxiety is an example). It is worth remembering, fearful people initiate measures to protect themselves.

One more important feature of the Deep Mind: it is a positive, problem solver by nature so it does not understand the concept, 'no'. It ignores it or, more frequently, automatically translates it into, 'yes'. Think about it, "Tommy, don't go next door to where the new family with the kids moved in." Yeah, sure. Ten minutes later . . . Or one for the reader: "Under NO circumstances think about a purple elephant." Additional support for the truth of it will be offered as we go along. (Nancy Reagan's, "Just Say No," campaign against drugs was, we see, doomed from the beginning.)

Think about that in terms of setting rules. Which, then, has a better chance of working (being accepted by our child's guidance system – the Deep Mind): "Do not hit your sister", or "Be kind and gentle with your sister like you want people to be with you?" Unfortunately, rules are typically stated as negatives (a Conscious Mind concept, quite foreign to the Deep Mind). It is why they are impossible to enforce without inflicting sever repercussions and are seldom followed once the person is away from the 'rule enforcer'. Again, more later. Suffice it to say, we all – especially kids – need to know what we *should* be doing to have a successful life, rather than what we *should not* be doing. "Don't hit," does not help the child learn what to do instead when he is frustrated, or angry, feels threatened or believes his rights have been violated. [Those interested in pursuing the topic may find my book, *The One Rule Plan for Family Happiness*, useful. Amazon ISBN: 978 1692598976]

Let me try it one more way: if a child learns to accept the value, *love*, (a positive value or a 'yes' value) there is little or no room left for its incompatible alternative, hate (a negative value). Think, every time a 'love card' is deposited in the Deep Mind its presence grows in terms of 'bulk and visibility'. Compare a Deep Mind containing 1000 love cards and ten hate cards with one containing 1000 hate cards and ten love cards.

Where the conscious mind runs on words and logic, the Deep Mind uses both words and logic *poorly*. It runs on emotions, images, close proximity, and correlation.

Experiences or ideas that enter the Deep Mind with great emotion attached to them are preserved front and center – believed above those accompanied by little emotion.

Consider how the Deep Mind deals with its experiences from learning and classroom environments as set up by these three teachers: one compassionate, one distant, and one who freely punishes. Compassion produces strong, positive emotion and approval (to learning, in this case). Lack of emotion produces uncertainty. Punishment produces strong, negative emotion (fear/dislike).

The Deep Mind assumes that ideas or experiences that enter it simultaneously or in close proximity, are to be connected forever. (The presence of a caterpillar and terror; love and understanding 'becomes' grandmother; the image of that teacher who offers praise when deserved and the child's positive feelings about learning; the arrival of father after work and the spankings he delivers at the mother's request.)

Experiences and ideas that enter the Deep Mind with an apparent cause and effect relationship maintain that perceived relationship. (If/then. If the light goes on when the switch is flipped, then the switch caused the light to go on – upon investigation, that is reasonable. If I failed a test after having oatmeal for breakfast means I must not eat oatmeal before a test – unreasonable to the conscious mind, but forever meaningful to the non-logical Deep mind. What about this one? When I express an idea my father doesn't like, he slaps me or puts me down? How might that affect my willingness to offer ideas – in general – in the future?)

Just a few more important things about the Deep Mind, and its crucial role in value development, then we will do a quick review and move on to consider the values and how they can save or destroy humanity – beginning at the levels of individuals and families.

As you have already found, the manner in which 'value beliefs' are set into the Deep Mind can have life-long consequences. Values of some nature *will* find their way into the

Deep Mind, so, it is the parents' responsibility to thoughtfully 'usher in' only those they believe will be helpful. (It's a ticklish task we will explore more thoroughly, as we proceed through the values.)

Ideas that are set into the Deep Mind most often, most recently or with the most emotion are most likely to be acted upon regularly. Let's say the Deep Mind holds two ideas – mother loves me, and mother hurts me. If a severe spanking just occurred, in which way will the Deep Mind be characterizing 'my mother' – *mother hurts me*. Not only was it the most recent, but it probably involved more intense emotion than the peck on the lad's forehead when he left for school that morning. In fact, the emotion associated with one spanking might outweigh two dozen, emotionally flat kisses as far as the Deep Mind is concerned. Remember, ultimately, the Deep Mind controls all our behavior and beliefs. (Also, I suppose, remember that corporal punishment is the physical equivalent of the verbal, 'NO'. Tender touch is the equivalent of the verbal – YES. Hmm? Perhaps we understand why no matter how often Adam gets beatings, he continues to misbehave.)

For the reader who is interested in learning much more about how the Deep Mind operates and how to go about rearranging and making positive changes in the directives it uses to guide a person, the reader can consult my book, *Deep Mind Mastery*. *1

For our purposes, here, we need to remember several things: habitual values reside in the Deep Mind. We call them Directives. The conscious mind doesn't know much about what's 'down there'. The ones that most regularly direct our behavior are those planted or re-planted (filed or refiled) there most frequently and most recently (practiced or used recently) along with those planted there accompanied by the largest doses of emotions. Praise for, and good outcomes from, demonstrating a value, re-sets it (moves its 'cards' further to the left).

For all of us, especially children, regularly practicing values that move humanity and society forward in loving and positive ways, helps assure those values will continue to guide us. Regularly wrapping those positive values in love and other intense, positive, emotions further ensures the likelihood it will be those that are acted upon – regularly referred to and used. Each time an idea or tendency for some behavior is repeated, it is reset with additional power in the Deep Mind. Resetting maintains it as the 'go to' tendency. (My mother saw to it that every time I left the house the values that made me a 'positive Tommy' were re-set.)

A person may claim to believe in peace and love, but unless his or her Deep Mind regularly receives plain and clear messages to that effect, they will move lower on the priority ladder of Deep Mind Directives making less than loving responses more possible (selfishness, for example). We have heard the term, 'He's better than that', indicating somebody behaved in a manner not typical of how we remembered him or knew him to be. In such a case we must suspect lack of recent practice or, even, the recent practice of some competing negative belief or behavior that the Deep Mind has reason to suspect was to be moved forward into the 'ready, rapid response' section. Threat or fear, perhaps.

Since the mind is consumed with millions of transactions every second, many of which are more than willing to replace the high priorities in our Deep Mind, we must make certain we regularly force it to deal with resetting those positive values we understand need to guide our approach to living. Exhibiting them through interpersonal relationships is the very best sort of resetting mechanism. The religion-based equivalent is the rip-roaring, highly emotional, Bible-thumping, sermon every Sunday morning (sort of).

Perhaps in addition to asking how school went, we should ask, 'What did you do today that made life better for somebody?" Or, instead of, "What are you going to be when you grow up," ask, "How are you going to make the world a better place when you grow up?"

Which children will be regularly directed by a set of positive social values, the ones from the family that spends Sunday afternoons doing helpful things for seniors and the infirmed, or the ones from the family that sits in front of the TV watching mindless movies or programs or playing video games that promote conflict or violence?

At this point, it is easy to understand why fearful, insecure, uninformed, folks are generally 'closed-minded', make less effort to get to know those who are different, are less inclined to be helpful to 'those who are not *us'*, and feel the need to keep what they have, thinking they might need it when things go wrong *for them* down the road. It is also easy to understand why confident, secure, well-informed, folks are generally 'open-minded', are eager to get to know those who are different, offer to help others without consideration of how similar or dissimilar they may be, and believe in sharing what they have in order to build a more equitable and compassionate society. *The dual powerhouses in our endeavor to save humanity: Education and Experience.*

It might be useful to look up the generic terms *conservative* and *liberal* (not the political parties) if one feels the need to attach labels to the two approaches. [There are always exceptions.] 'Closed' and 'Open' approaches to social interaction begin and end with the Directives one's Deep Mind holds and attends to. 'Closed' tends to damage and destroy the human species – if not by direct attack, at least by omission. 'Reasonably Open' tends to enhance and preserve the human species.

Rules and *values* lead to very different behaviors. *Rules* are set by others, typically established with no input from those who must follow them. That makes them somebody else's dictate, not mine – I haven't had to buy into them as right or best; I just have to follow them. When he who established the rules also has power to enforce them – *enforce* typically implies punishment or negative consequences when they are broken – the one who must adhere to them will typically only feel compelled to follow them when the one with power to punish is present or is likely to hear about a trespass. In fewer words – Rule compliance typically follows the principle, out of sight/out of mind.

This is the important difference!

Values are grown *within the person* because they have been demonstrated to provide the best guidance to make life go well for all concerned. "I act some way because I want to and see the merit in it, not because I am forced to." Values represent – have been proven to be – the most dependable guidance system.

Kids from 'Rule' families frequently go to pieces when they leave home. Kids from 'Value' families almost always do quite well. (Take it from an old psychologist who has witnessed both hundreds of times.)

Values are portable and go with and guide a person wherever he or she goes. Rules are only situational and hold little or no 'power' once out of site of the enforcer. (Speeding when no cop is present?)

In the beginning, values are acquired by watching the 'modeling' of those values and seeing how valuable they are. Children don't learn values by being told what values to hold (organized religion has always had that wrong). Regular modeling, in form and results, is essential. The one clear certainty in child rearing is, 'Children learn most completely what they see and feel, not what they hear.' (You see the immediate connection to Deep Mind processing.)

Children are already learning the basics of *values at the level of feelings* while they still recline helplessly in their little beds – am I regularly attended to and am I treated gently with love and compassion, are my needs met immediately and regularly, am I always safe and protected, is my air clean and easy to breath, am I regularly and tenderly touched and held as if I am a part of my caretakers. In other words, is this world taking good care of me? Children begin acquiring and evaluating impressions and 'feelings' about their world, their people, and themselves from their first days of life. Babies love to be talked to in gentle, 'googoo' language – not because they understand the meaning of the words but because of the gentle, reassuring tone and the positive attention. And what does the Deep Mind run on – feelings, not words. Just imagine all the Deep Mind Directives the infant has already acquired by the time he or she first manages to roll over. (For what it's worth, baby's hear high tones best – the mother's voice – the falsetto, 'googoo gaga language' actually has some merit.)

What will take place in the remaining pages of this book?
Two dozen Positive Social Values will be presented and discussed in relation to the opposite of each, the Harmful Social Values. Remember, a Positive Social Value is one that generally contributes to a helpful, growth producing, person-valuing, individual and society. Harmful social values are generally destructive and do the opposite.

Bottom line: A society overtaken by people harboring and acting on harmful social values (greed and hate, for example) will contribute to the demise – the extinction – of the human species. Students of human history have accumulated ample examples of how it has occurred on smaller scales.

As the title of this book suggests, what the author is going for, here, is nothing short of saving humanity by building lives based in the regular, active, demonstration of Positive Social Values.

SUMMARY OF
DEEP MIND (DM) FUNCTIONS

The DM controls virtually all human behavior.

It is typically hidden from the conscious mind.

There are well-established methods for appropriately accessing and tending to the DM.

It uses words poorly. Where the Conscious Mind runs on words and logic, the DM relies, *instead*, on images, correlation, emotions, recency and frequency of events.

The DM is completely nonjudgmental. It believes whatever it thinks *it's person* has told it. Therefore, it has no problem holding incompatible alternatives at the same time. [My person loves, my person hates, my person doesn't care, can all be present. Which are most likely to be rolled out for use: the ones that have been set most freq----ly, the ones set with the most p----ful em----n, and have been set most rec---ly.]

The DM does not understand the concept, 'No', and either ignores it or treats it as if were, 'Yes'. The DM often treats punishment like it treats the verbal, 'no'. (The, "I'll show you", reaction.)

What it believes, are called *Directives* – powerful setters and directors of behaviors. [Other models of the human mind use different terms.]

The DM is, first of all, a problem solver, it never sleeps, and works tirelessly to find *some* answer to the questions it believes its person has asked. (Who was that blond that sat in front of me in Senior English? Four hours later up it pops as if out of nowhere – Mary Ann Caudle – thanks to the tireless Deep Mind searching through billions of memories for you as you went about your life.)

Things like values that reside there, must be practiced, or at least recalled frequently to make sure they are the ones most readily available when its person is called upon to act or react. Those that are unused, work themselves to the lesser important end of the line.

Deep Minds that frequently absorb (feel, or visualize,

actually) that their person is good and capable and respected and loveable, provide the best guides for constructive behavior and happy, well-adjusted lives. Those that absorb the opposite will work overtime to prove their person is bad, incapable, selfish, hurtful, and untrustworthy. The DM believes what it hears about its person. One, highly emotional put down, can outweigh dozens of mildly offered positive comments or experiences. (I can describe many dozens of situations in which one, traumatizing remark from a parent or important person, has caused debilitating maladjustment.)

The first kernels of positive or harmful social values begin being set into the DM from shortly after birth from the nature and quality of the child's interactions with its world.

Here is an exercise I think will be helpful. Let me describe a 'value' program I initiated in a cottage of six boys, living together in what back then was called an orphanage. Think about it in terms of what we have reviewed so far.

Each morning at breakfast, each boy drew a card from a deck of 'values' - kindness, altruism, respect and so on. For the rest of that day, during their regular pursuits, they were to 'spread it around'. At supper they reported how it went – what worked and what didn't work so well and how they felt about it. They made suggestions to each other. The next morning, they drew cards again and off they went to improve their world with a new assignment. (It should work over a families breakfast table, as well.)

Analyze the 'program' in terms of what you have learned about the Deep Mind. What things was the program trying to accomplish and how were the Deep Mind principals incorporated? [That was dependably a question on tests in my Adolescent Psychology classes when I taught at the State University of New York, National College of Education, and Winston Churchill College.]

[Note: some readers may question some of my proposals or view of the facts or suppositions. That is fine. Demonstrate with *facts* how my words are questionable. I will revel in that. I may be old, but not too old to grow!]

----

1 Deep Mind Mastery, 2013, Tom Gnagey, The Family of Man Press, Amazon ASIN: B00F5H832U

SECTION TWO

Values: here we come

Setting the Stage

In this section, several dozen pairs of Simple Values – a socially positive value and its socially negative counterpart – will be presented. Each set will be illustrated, discussed, means for implementation will be suggested, and a conclusion stated relative to why it is important that the positive version is accepted as the habitual approach to living – the one that has the best chance of saving humanity from self-destruction.

Most of the Illustrations have been drawn from my experiences during the past eighty years, so consider them my best reconstructions. I figure if I am going to suggest a set of principles, the least I can do is provide real life examples from my real life – ones I should understand. The pairs are presented in no particular order – set twenty is as important in its way as set one. The reader will notice that several value sets are similar in nature, but both are included because folks typically characterize them in one or the other of those ways. Mankind probably cannot have too many positive values and this list is certainly not to be considered complete. You will want to add some of your own and do your own assessment in the manner I have done below. A few 'extra pairs' are listed at the end for your consideration and practice if you want.

My hope is that the readers will approach the information and ideas presented with open minds during the first read through. Save the more meticulous analysis for later. The openness I'm hoping for will ask: What does this book say that just might have some merit?)

Getting Down to Work

The SOCIAL VALUES

(The positive/helpful value is stated first, and the negative/harmful value, second)

VALUE PAIR ONE:
Logical problem-solving techniques
rather than
physical aggression

The Illustration

I was twelve and had just entered eighth grade in a new school, far larger than I was used to. The school policy was to 'hold back' students who failed subjects. I found among my classmates six who had been held back more than once – sixteen-year-old eighth grade 'men', who outweighed me by twice and stunk like a locker room.

In my previous school, I had already had four years of science classes. In my new school, science didn't enter the curriculum until eighth grade, so I was way ahead. I made A's on all the tests – we had one every Friday. The 'boy-men' took it upon themselves to try and intimidate me into doing more poorly on those tests – 'So their curve could go up' (Clearly budding statisticians.) They took to pounding on my left shoulder throughout the days until it was permanently black and blue – and sore – soooo sore.

My parents were newly retired educators. I could not just begin failing the tests. It was a dilemma. I felt I needed to handle it myself and not burden my folks who suddenly had enough new things to contend with. I confided in a new friend.

"They're jealous because you're smart and they're dumb.

They also hate you because you're a Yankee. That's probably mostly it."

He figured he had it solved. Maybe he had, but that didn't do anything to assure me I would grow to adulthood with two functioning arms. What he said sparked an idea. I took James aside – the least aggressive and probably brightest of the lot – and told him I'd make him a bet that if he let me help him study, I'd promise him at least a 'C' on the next week's test. There were two provisos: he didn't dare tell anybody what was going on between us and, if his grade improved according to my promise, he would stop hitting me. I understood that nothing I knew about him made me believe he'd abide by his side of the bargain, but still, I pursued it – it was what I had.

He agreed and we met for a half hour before school each day. I was amazed at how little he knew about studying – well, telling it like it was, he knew *nothing* about studying. How could a school have not taught that??? I discovered he read poorly, so I read the chapter to him while he followed along. Like I did when I was reading to myself, I would stop periodically and ask questions. I made sure he knew the answers before we went on. I could tell he was getting into it – he'd show up before I did.

Friday morning before First Period Science, I helped him review one last time. Class came to order. The tests were handed out. We all went to work on them. I noticed Mrs. Rice took note of how hard he was working. That was clearly out of character for him. It was worth a private smile. He was the last to hand in his paper – it was hard to take a written test when you couldn't read. Like usual, I had been the first.

The weekend came and went. I managed to avoid the 'black and blue gang'. It was the teacher's practice to hand back the test papers first, and then take a few minutes to go through the questions as a final review of the material. Before she began that morning, she asked the class, "What could be the biggest surprise about these test scores?"

"That Tommy (me) failed!"

There was lots of laughter. The boy beside me thumped my back in a show of comradery – maybe admiration.

"Well, *almost* as unbelievable, James made a B+."

The room fell silent. In slow motion, mouths agape, everybody turned toward him. He grinned. He held up his paper so everybody could see that the teacher's pronouncement was, in fact, true. I did my best to contain my pleasure. He managed a wink in my direction. I returned it with a subdued thumbs up.

James kept *half* his bargain – he never hit me again. Tuesday morning, however, six, giant, stink factories arrived with Barry for our study session on the next chapter. I told them I'd help them on the condition they'd bathe before they came. I am pleased to report my arm is fully functional to this day, although I find it useful to tell myself that my poor typing skills are directly connected to that first month in eighth grade.

Months later, at the End-of-the-year Awards Ceremony, I received the 'Best Citizen' award – a first for a boy in that school I was told. I wasn't even embarrassed when seven, huge, sweet smelling associates stood and clapped and cheered and whistled and stomped their feet at the rear of the auditorium. I had to smile thinking that in no more than six years they would probably be graduating from high school and I would return to do the same for them. (Three dropped out, but two made it in four – really! They learned stuff once they believed they could learn stuff.)

I gained an appreciation of the disadvantaged learner and, perhaps influenced by them, spent a significant portion of my early adult life working to help students with learning problems benefit more significantly from the educational process. Often, it was altering the educational process so the students could benefit from it.

The Discussion

It was, perhaps, fortuitous that I was outnumbered, so fighting back was never really on the table. Anyway, it was not how we settled things in my home. We used our heads. We were problem solvers. At supper we often played a game I called *Escape*. 'If you were trapped inside a ________ (saltshaker, lion's den, etc.), how would you escape?' We would think it through together. It typically became hilarious. When I went to my parents with a problem, they helped me think it through, with a nudge here and there, offering little out and out advice. I always came away with a plan or new perspective. Grampa once told me, "Life is little more than solving problems – the better problem solver/avoider you are, the better life you will have." I had to wonder, if what he said were true, why didn't schools teach classes in problem solving?

People with poor problem-solving skills are often forced

into corners. One way to escape dangerous corners is to fight your way out. Those who must rely on physical aggression rather than problem solving are a danger to our survival, both as individuals and as a species.

The Implementation

As we move along, you may become tired of hearing this premise: Start a child along the path toward logical problem solving early in his life. We help him discover the necessary elements. Provide lots of practice. We help him understand that having a problem becomes a good thing – another chance to practice solving it and learn new things. When a child's mental skills are still primitive, we merely help him understand problems can be solved, therefore, he should bring them to our attention so he can learn what to do about them. For the toddler that might mean, take the wayward shoe to mom rather than throw it across the room – one of those methods solves the problem; the other doesn't. He must come to understand that. Our plan becomes more sophisticated as the child matures.

The Conclusion

Confronting a problem with unbridled, physical force, seldom works as well as logical problem solving. The first leaves destruction, unresolved anger, and unsolved issues in its wake – not a way to save mankind. The second not only avoids unnecessary confrontation, but it has a good chance of being helpful and growing the mind as it practices. Also, it demonstrates the good sense of asking for help – finding and utilizing reliable resources.

* * * * *

VALUE PAIR TWO:
Accepting others as they are
rather than
trying to change them

ILLUSTRATION:

It was my first counseling session with a brilliant nine-year-old – Zackery – never Zack or Zacky. He was smart enough to see the big problems in the world but had too little real-life information and wisdom to solve them. It was a terribly frustrating situation for him. That was why his parents thought they had brought him to visit with me. Zackery, however, believed the more pressing need in his life was learning how to deal with the 'Dumb majority' he felt himself encountering every day.

"You will find I am very smart, but even so, I cannot understand why people are constructed like they are. I will need to explain that to you," (me being one the 'Dumb majority', I figured).

I smiled and nodded for him to continue.

"Here's how I have it figured," he went on. "I believe the use of a metaphor I have been using inside my head is the best way of describing the situation. People are like sponges. They absorb the experiences that come their way in life – usually pretty much like they really are but often their perceptions and therefore their memories are influenced by what they *don't* understand. That requires them to fill in those parts with lore they make up to complete the scene or idea. Did you get that?"

Did I mention he was brilliant?

"I believe I am following you. Go on."

He nodded with some relief. Perhaps, I had just moved up to the 'Not quite so dumb majority'.

"The contents of a person's sponge is, therefore, only obvious to him – it remains hidden from the rest of us. Outsiders cannot know what another's sponge has picked up and carries with it."

He paused as if his conundrum should be obvious. It wasn't. I could feel a demotion in my near future.

"It's true. Our fund of experiences is unique to each of us. Some tend to share more of it than others."

I hoped that would move him to continue thinking out loud.

"You are urging me to continue. Okay. I can come to know anything I choose to set my mind to except the contents of other people's sponges and that pisses me off, greatly."

"Are you saying they don't have a right to their privacy?"

"I don't see why. I could be of far greater service to them if I had a more accurate way of reading their sponge."

"You believe it is your job to fix other people's sponges?"

"Somebody clearly needs to. People do really dumb things and then tend to repeat them over and over again."

"They might call that their right or need for privacy."

"Just stupidity, when I could fix them if I could just observe their sponges."

"So, you are telling me there is nothing in *your* sponge you wouldn't feel happy to share with the whole world?"

I got a look – somewhere between puzzlement and terror. He looked away. There was a l o n g silence. Gradually, he began to nod. He returned his gaze toward my face.

"I will tell my parents that you earned your outrageous fee today. You have made the well-taken point that we each have the right to the privacy of our sponges. Not efficient, probably even deadly, but I get the point. That further implies that it is not my responsibility to change people even though the version I'd make of them would be vastly superior.

"It will be a new way of life for me – accepting others the pathetic way they are rather than changing them into how I believe they could or should be. That will not be easy for me. I have always figured I knew what's best for everybody – well, I do. That doesn't change. In a way, it is quite a relief – takes a huge burden off my shoulders – such as they are on a nine-year-old boy."

I thought he was leading up to smile. He wasn't.

He stood, signaling the session was over. He reached out to shake my hand – a ninety-year-old man in a nine-year-old body.

"Thank you. Same time next week. We need to consider the marbles people keep in their cheeks."

The lad was a walking encyclopedia of esoteric metaphors.

In the waiting room he addressed his parents.

"I must admit you were right to have dragged me here and I was wrong about wanting to run away screaming into the dark. And, oh, in the future, I will leave your sponges alone."

His parents and I exchanged shrugs.

Eventually, the lad would teach me almost as much as I taught him. Our sponges became pretty good friends that next few months. I think we were both better because of the time we spent together. If nothing else, his cheeks learned to smile and his voice box, to chuckle.

Another experience:

One of the most important lessons I learned during my 'psychologist life' came from a 14-year-old foster son. He was from a 'socially disadvantaged' home to which, hopefully, he would eventually be able to return. He was bright, an avid pool player, and didn't fit well into a traditional school setting. He seemed to take some pleasure in mimicking the language style my wife and I spoke. He became quite good at it – in social settings he could pass himself off as a member of our family with ease.

I said something dumb to him like, "I'm proud of the way your English is coming around. What do other people say about it?"

I got a look that implied, "How dumb can you be, Doc?"

He provided an immediate response.

"If I talked like you do back in my home or at the pool hall, they'd never let me come back."

I understood it was an overstatement, but it brought an important truth home to me both as a young psychologist and a foster father – be very careful what you meddle with in others – there are people out there who should NOT be like you are. It was a life-changing realization that immediately made me a more effective instrument of change.

DISCUSSION:

You may have found the fallacy in this Positive Value – *don't try to change others.* The secondary point of this book (the first being to make a case for Positive Social Values) is to help others come to accept and live according to those values. That might involve changing them as people. I'll give this rationalization for my point here: requiring a mate to wear green instead of her preferred, brown, is just not the same as me offering possibilities and suggestions for the readers' consideration about saving the world from destruction. (Discuss among friendly sponges, if you want.)

Diversity is a powerful positive force in the lives of human beings. Contemplating it forces evaluation – could that be of benefit to me? A world of clones would mean there would be no individuality. Think about your characteristics that set you apart from others – things you like and flaunt and then things you may not like and hide. You have the right to demonstrate and enjoy all those elements that make you the you that you like, providing none are harmful to yourself or others. (Five *you's* in one sentence, there – do *you* suppose that's close to a record?)

The value also implies that not only do we allow others to be themselves, but we work to be comfortable with that – pleased they are able to be who and what and how they prefer to be. Our job is not to judge, but to observe. If we decide someone's set of traits is not attractive to us, we are free to move on and find someone with whom we can be comfortable. Of course, if their traits are harmful to themselves or the rest of us, then protective measures must be taken.

IMPLICATIONS:

History suggests, if not proves, that societies that have boasted diversity among their citizens tend to be robust; *it takes a million different stars to make a proper night sky – some bright, some dim, some big, some small.*

That was a quote from a smelly old man who let me ride beside him on his manure spreader as he made his rounds in my little town – my hero as a four-year-old. Many of the ladies in our church would have liked to change him – clean him up, take soap and water to both him and the grubby, encrusted, wide, floorboards in his hut. Even as a tyke I couldn't understand that. He was just about the happiest person I had ever known. He would never hurt anybody. During the summer, he and I took his garden wares around to old people and poor people and sick people – some to the very ladies who wanted to change him. He never charged anybody and always left them anonymously on their porches and pledged me to silence about it all. (Shhh!) I got it that other's disliked his aroma, but since he disliked being with others it really was not a problem.

If everybody who wanted to change something about that old man had gotten to do it, there would have been nobody left inside him. Grampa called the people who spent their energy disparaging him, the *Holier than Thou Brigade*. I just called them thoughtless and mean. Not a one of them knew anything about who he really was. I even knew a saying about it: Before you criticize somebody, walk a day in their shoes. I have to admit, I was the only boy I knew who ever really tried to do that, right up there on that seat behind his mules. (I often wondered how mother knew I had been with him!)

CONCLUSION:

When a person feels the need to change another person relative to his lesser traits, it probably says more about the insecurity of the one promoting the changes than about the other person. It can become a good, growth changing exercise to contemplate why one needs to be in control of others in that way. It may, also, be revealing of one's own personal traits that are making the Deep Mind uncomfortable. In general, the world is a better place when we attend to improving ourselves rather than changing others. The natural reaction of a person who is forced to be somebody he really isn't, is anger. A world of changed but angry folks is not going to save humanity.

* * * * *

VALUE PAIR THREE:
Universal dignity among men
rather than
Self-righteous bigotry

ILLUSTRATION:

This one is closely tied to the previous one and may seem like an odd pairing. Hear me out.

Some months ago, on a city bus, I found myself next to a five-year-old black boy who was sitting between his grandmother and me. I chatted with her. The boy was listening but seemed silently concerned with other matters.

Presently . . .

"Your skin is white."

I held my arm out next to his.

"It is – just a pale, washed out white, not bold and beautiful like yours."

He spent some time thinking about our exchange, then . . .

"Yeah, it *is* beautiful. White people don't like me because it's black."

"I like it and you, and I'm an old white guy."

He thought some more as he studied my face. Something really important was going on inside him. I waited.

"I think you are white on the outside and black on the inside."

"Wouldn't that be wonderful!"

"It is. I'm pretty sure."

He nodded up into his grandmother's face for her reassurance. I'm sure he didn't understand her single tear.

I learned about his baby sister and his skateboard and going to school on his computer and . . .

In the end I got a wonderful hug – well, two, actually.

DISCUSSION:

I posted this story on Face Book and immediately received

35

an outpouring of kind words. I also received one blistering response informing me that I was going to Hell for spreading such dangerous trash about racial equality. (If true, I expect to find a lot of really nice people in Hell.)

The happy side of the experience is obvious. The sad side is that in order to trust me and relate to me, the boy had to make me like him – part black – because he knew a white man couldn't be treating a black boy kindly. The experience took place in Arkansas, USA. There are many wonderful, open, accepting folks here. There are many who harbor generations old prejudice against those with non-white skin color. These 'different' looking folks become easy scapegoats for a person's own shortcomings. When you believe the color of your skin makes you innately superior to all people whose skin is some other color, and you see yourself not doing as well as you would like, it is easy (helpful) to have such a group to blame. 'They take jobs I should have.' 'Because they are lazy, they take benefits paid for by my taxes.' Why are *they* bad people, again: 'Because they're black.' And on and on.

I was about six, standing in line at a carnival with my fourteen-year-old brother. I had never seen a black man, but there I was standing beside one. My friends said they all carried knives and slit white boys' throats. I reached out with my index finger and touched his arm. He looked down at me and offered the greatest smile I'd ever seen. I nodded up at him. He nodded down at me. I was never afraid of black men again. It's fascinating how one small positive exchange can change another's life forever. I try to initiate such encounters frequently – like the boy on the bus.

Prejudice immediately and automatically divides people into *us* (the desirables) and *them* (those with less innate dignity, the undesirables – more likely, the *dangerous* undesirables). Actually, that stems from a normal and necessary function of the human mind. Remember, the prime directive of the Deep Mind is to keep its person safe – alive, not dead. When it cannot be fully certain that someone is safe to be with, it has to characterize him as unsafe until facts prove otherwise – it won't take even the smallest chance it might be in danger.

Prejudice separates groups. The only sure way to become convinced a 'different' group is safe, is to mix with them, get to know them, come to trust them. Prejudice – the ultimate separator – makes that sense of safety and comfort, impossible, as it insists on the distance and turns the initial uncertainty into fact. Ultimately, what is the surest way to make certain a 'dangerous' group does not negatively impact or destroy 'your' group? Destroy it (or at least these days, keep it from voting). Prejudice can be characterized as the outward manifestation of hate.

Insecure folks are easily frightened and are not likely to seek out and examine individual members of 'different' groups, while secure and inquisitive folks find safe ways of 'finding out'. That tends to answer the question about why liberals (inquisitive, accepting, and open by dictionary definition) are many times less likely to exhibit prejudice than the less liberal (less secure and therefore more closed). Prejudice plus ignorance combine to proliferate the problem through generations.

I have often wished that, as a grown up, I could speak with that black man at the carnival and let him know how his kindly response to the little white kid, changed my life.

IMPLEMENTATION:

The fact is that if a person believes some other person or group is a danger to his happiness or survival he will, at the least forceful level, avoid them – at the most forceful level, destroy them. My adopted state has a terribly sad history of lynching 'the different'. To turn that around for the long term, mingling – mutual participation – must be encouraged. It starts from the time a child begins to interact with others. It is reinforced by what the child hears at home and what he sees his parents do. People who know each other and enjoy and feel safe in each other's company are most unlikely to disrespect each other or kill each other off. Libraries are wonderful places in that respect – everybody's ok, everybody's accepted, everybody's due respect and eager assistance. I love libraries; perhaps our new melting pot. [When you come to *Value # Twenty-Five* below you will examine another example of how this worked in my life.]

CONCLUSION:

A world divided because of misunderstanding due to the ignorance that accompanies the lack of social interaction makes mutual trust and cooperation nearly impossible. Since solving the big problems that will destroy mankind demand universal cooperation and trust, the separation that is encouraged – forced – by prejudice, makes prejudice one of the most serious forces leading to the destruction of mankind. We must always shoot for universal dignity and inclusion if the survival of mankind is important to us.

I'm not sure if this is where this illustration fits, but it's just too darn cute to omit.

On a bench at Walmart, I was chatting with a mother and her daughter (maybe six) visiting from India. In a lull in the conversation the girl patted my arm and said, "I just love your accent!"

* * * * *

VALUE PAIR FOUR:
Cooperative approach
rather than
an unbridled competitive approach.

ILLUSTRATION:

Hank was eleven. I was ten. We both had push mowers (in 1947 that meant no motor). We both mowed lawns for summer spending money. I began having unexplained problems with my mower – a loose wheel, a chipped blade. A story was circulated that I couldn't be trusted because my mower was falling apart – I lost one lawn to Hank because of it.

I asked around. Hank was behind the rumor. He was approaching my clients and trying to talk them into switching to him. One night, I left my mower in clear view on the narrow walk beside my house. I hid where I could keep an eye on it that evening. As I suspected, Hank came along and messed with it – stole the wooden roller. I told dad and asked for a suggestion. Our discussions were often more abstract than immediately practical.

"I think you can handle this one, Tommy. Maybe this might be a good starting place; we've spoken of it before in other contexts. Remember our conversations about how cooperation usually makes for a better life than competition?"

I did remember. I figured I mostly understood where he was leading me. Developing such a lead myself was always more fun than if he had just told me what to do.

It was the second week in June. I figured we had about the same number of lawns – maybe six each. I chatted him up.

"Hope your lawn business is going good. You've got a great mower. I've almost got more requests than I can handle. Was wondering if you'd want to go into business together – we could add a few more and back each other up – split the money according to how many hours we each worked each week. We could cover for each other when there were other things one of us wanted to do. The next day he came over and we worked out an agreement – I wrote it down and we both signed it.

The arrangement worked quite well. I typed up fifty business cards and we left them with folks who clearly neglected their lawns. Hank's older sister handled the phone calls. I talked our mayor (and barber – it was a tiny town) into having a *'Best Kept Lawn'* contest as part of our annual, 'Kraut and Sausage Festival' coming up in August. By mid-July we had hired another boy to help part time. We finished our final lawns for the season on September 15th, school had been in session two weeks.

After school, Hank and I celebrated over a malted at the drug store. We talked about our business and made plans for the following summer. We would expand our services to planting and caring for flower gardens (another contest, and therefore more work for us, I was sure). We could hire our helper full time. I never confronted him about his hijinks early in the summer. It stopped, of course. That had originally been the point of my plan – I couldn't pull my weight in the partnership if my machine weren't in tiptop condition. Early on, he managed to 'stumble across' a wooden roller, virtually identical to the one I had lost.

DISCUSSION:

In *cooperation*, folks work out a mutually facilitating arrangement. That means everybody wins. In *competition*, folks work to always best the others. That means somebody – most everybody, really – always loses. In the set of values I had learned in my home, *helping* underscored most everything. *Hurting* was a sin in the religious-speak of the conservative church in which I was raised. I later translated 'good and evil' into continuums such as appropriate to not appropriate, growth producing to growth stunting, helpful to hurtful, and so on. Clearly, early on, in his attempt to compete with me and better me, Hank resorted to hurtful activities. In some quarters, highly competitive folks are characterized as selfish – wanting to get the best of everybody – hog the glory for themselves. That's neither here nor there for our purposes. The point is, in the case of Hank and me, cooperation worked wonders for both of us. We still didn't like each other much, but we learned to be comfortable with each other.

Contrary to the often-touted advantage for the consumer, the law of supply and demand often tends to take advantage of the consumer. It is really 'seller centered' – set to be in the seller's best interest – rather than 'consumer centered' as it would be in a cooperative based economy. He who sells at the lowest price may sell the most and therefore make the most money, but the basic goal is to run the competition out of business, then raise the prices.

IMPLEMENTATION:

Early in my career, I found myself at a convention of noted scientists. I had the opportunity to spend a few minutes, alone, with several dozen of them relative to a paper I was working on. One question I put to each of them was: Why have you spent your life doing what you have done? To a person, their responses indicated their motivation had nothing to do with fame or money – it was the problem and the search and the discovery that were important – the benefits to mankind. That pretty well shot the implication from the 'competition advocates' that without the spirit of competition, science (any important endeavor) would eventually fall by the wayside. Their theory is the only reason one strives to accomplish anything is fame and fortune that comes with being first or best. I met not one scientist who indicated glory as a motivator. Leaders in most fields that contribute to improving the human condition are motivated by the experience and the feelings of personal achievement – the positive contribution it will make. [The reader may want to contrast that with politics, finance, entertainment, applied medicine, business, and professional sports.]

It nullifies the idea that without competition, society will crumble. It is a theory mostly pushed by unfortunate folks who are primarily led by their own greed and huge egos and the constant need to have them stroked. Greed is a kind of need to win, isn't it?

Cooperative groups – families, churches, clubs, societies – thrive in all the necessary positive ways, while overly competitive groups destroy each other – after all, the goal of serious competition is to be the best, the one and only, thereby putting everybody else out of contention.

Encourage cooperation in children. It builds strong, positive bonds with others as well as a sense of safety. It highlights how others are important in your life. Competition is divisive and fosters the 'us against them' mentality. Cooperation is inclusive. I once did the math in a regional basketball tournament – 400 boys began, a team of ten won – 390 boys lost. One MVP – 399 lost. Hmm.

Which has the best chance of helping our species live on?

* * * * *

VALUE PAIR FIVE:
Ability to delay gratification
rather than
the need for immediate gratification.

ILLUSTRATION:

Back in my early, 'psychologist' days, I had a group of four, twelve-year-old boys referred by their teacher because she feared the values and beliefs they held would be the cause of sorrow for them and others in the future. ("Jailbirds by 19," I believe actually represented her gentlest description.) They shared the, 'I want it *now* so I'll do whatever it takes to get it *now*', approach to organizing and running their lives.

At the outset, I tried my usual approach – listing several pairs of values, one likely to produce positive outcomes in one's life and one likely to produce harmful outcomes. Typically, I led them to think through the most likely end result of each – the idea being to let them characterize each and discover why life would be better if they would adopt the positive one. It usually worked well. (See chapter twelve in my novel, *Envisaging an Ideal Society: Lenonia rises out of chaos,* in which that technique is illustrated at length: Amazon ASIN : B016P4KITM)

These easily distracted boys would not engage in the exercise in a meaningful way, so I invented a card game – *Save or Spend©* There were two decks of cards, one referred to as, *'Paycheck'*, the second, *'Products'*. Each Paycheck card had a value of $1.00 printed on it. Each Product card showed some item of interest to boys that age and ranged in price from fifty cents to five dollars. Eight Product Cards, drawn randomly from the deck of many, were laid out face up in the center. Step one: each boy was dealt one Paycheck Card. Step two: alternating around the circle, each boy choose to buy a product or save his money for later. When he bought, his Paycheck(s) went back into the Paycheck deck. When he choose to save it to spend later, it went into his bank (stayed face up in front of him). Whenever a product card was purchased, the buyer picked it up and another randomly drawn product card was laid down in its place.

Each time the 'circle' was completed, they each received a new Paycheck card.

No winners or losers were declared. The only result was their private evaluation of how well the game went for them. They were asked to talk about their result. No appraisal was offered except, perhaps, from the others (gentle, unsolicited remarks such as, "You idiot!")

To my delight, the card game clearly nudged the boy's behavior – at least during the games – toward the positive value (delay gratification) and thus the associated positive behaviors. In institutional settings, 'real' products have been used – gum, treats, books, yard time, extra shower, etc. That seems to make carry-over changes in behavior. Promising!

For the original four boys, things happened like, forgo the laugh a boy could present to disrupt class in order to avoid missing recess because of it. That is a substantial insight for an impulsive 12-year-old.

In that original iteration of the game, the teacher (knowing nothing about the use of or nature of the game) reported obvious positive changes in the four boys' behavior eventually setting them up to discuss the problem itself.

There is no lesson learned better than the one learned from oneself. That saying may have come from my grandfather, or my father, or me. At my age, memories get jumbled and sometimes tend to make me look better than I probably was! (I know, it's hard to believe that I could possibly look better than I am!)

[Values Five and Six are closely connected. I chose to make two presentations, but to combine the discussion at the end of Value Six]

VALUE PAIR SIX:
A save and pay as you go approach,
rather than
irresponsible spend & credit approach.

ILLUSTRATION:

Growing up, my family's financial situation was never discussed with the children. Dad was a teacher, mother a housewife. We had what we needed plus a few extras. I never felt deprived and, as a six-year-old, enjoyed the life my ten cents a week allowance provided me – a penny went to church and a penny into our family help jar – money we kept on hand to help out those in need. The other eight cents were all mine. When I was six, my brothers – 14 and 16 – each received a quarter – that seemed fair. Billy, my oldest brother, spent most of his on girls – an inconceivable pursuit to me. Larry, my middle brother, sometimes bought me things – an orange sherbet cup with a wooden spoon, or a gumball out of the big, glass globe at *Chuck's Filling Station*. He made it seem right that, being younger, I should not spend mine on him.

Often, by Wednesday my dime was long gone. Larry always saved some of his in the mason jar on the stand next to his bed. We shared a room. One day after school I noticed his jar was empty. I took it downstairs to alert mother to the problem.

"Larry has been saving his money a long time so he could buy a ball glove. There's no problem."

I was amazed. The concept of me saving money for future purchases had never entered my mind. The process made immediate sense to me although the necessary problem caused more than a little reluctance – if I saved it, I didn't have it to spend.

There was one expensive item I really wanted – a Tom Mix Decoder Ring. It required two cereal box tops and twenty-five

45

cents. I talked it over with mother. She said if I agreed to eat the cereal until it was gone, she would buy the cereal for me. I would have to save or earn the money for the ring. During the following three weeks I saved eleven cents and earned fifteen helping Mr. Scaggs clean out his attic. (Interestingly, I learned my dad and brothers suddenly liked that cereal, as well. I grew up in a household of good people.)

I felt a new sort of pride – power, really – when I presented the twenty-five cents to mother so she could fix the envelope – address it, add the stamp, slip the box tops inside and tape a quarter to a sheet of paper with my name and address. She trusted me to take it to the Post Office by myself – a five block walk one way.

The next two weeks dragged on. I had periods with visions of a single dip cone when I questioned if I had made the right decision about it.

The afternoon it happened, however, it burned like a birthday candle into my memory. I arrived home after school. My routine was to go right to the kitchen, take a seat at the table, mom would pour a glass of milk and she and I would have a chat while she began preparing supper. I took my seat and found myself puzzled by the thick envelope there beside my milk.

"What's this?"

"Read what's on the envelope."

She pointed.

"*Here is the Tom Mix Secret Decoder Ring you have been waiting for. Guard it well and use it to get your secret messages directly from your favorite cowboy, Tom Mix.*" (She helped me with some of the words.)

My memory of the next half hour has faded. I do remember sitting on the living room floor in front of the big radio, waiting for his program to come on. I had paper and a pencil I had sharpened three times to make sure it was ready. Then came the code: T-1, G-7, P-3 and so on. I had by then figured out how to use it. I began the decoding. I hoped the message was just for me, but I couldn't be sure about that. *"Tomorrow, JAKE BLACK steals Tom's saddle bags."*

'Wow! I knew something none of my friends knew.'

I was ready to begin saving to get the glow in the dark arrowhead, complete with compass, from *Golden Arrow*, my Indian hero who, galloped out of his secret cave, riding his golden palomino, and caught all the bad guys who dared find their ways onto his radio program. Saving became a way of life – even, sometimes, when I didn't know what I was saving for. (Suddenly, my allowance jumped to fifteen cents. I neither understood that nor questioned it.)

I am getting close to losing faith in Superman, however. I have not yet received the *Superman's Greatest Adventure* record, I ordered in 1944. (I guess you gotta be leery of those men of steel.)

And, eventually, there was that $125 dollars I saved back from my Lifeguarding earnings that bought a diamond ring for the love of my life.

DISCUSSION:

These days, children seldom see the save first/pay less later approach to living. Instead, the typical experience is the buy now/pay more later approach. It promotes and condones impulsivity. It inhibits and discourages learning the ability to delay gratification. That greatly reduces one's financial position over the years and tends to keep poor people poor and middle-class people never more than a month or so away from financial collapse – bankruptcy. With no savings to fall back on for emergencies, new loans (and more interest) must be secured. The more debt a regular guy has the higher the interest rate will be charged. A good rule would probably be, aside from home and vehicle, save and pay cash. (The financial world would probably collapse.)

Impulsive behavior of any kind precludes one's ability to think through the ramifications – how will that behavior or response really affect my life down the road. It almost never adds quality to life. "Let's see, I only bought what I could pay for this year. Now, what will I do with the $1,000 I saved in interest (not to mention the actual money I saved by not making unnecessary or foolish, spur of the minute, purchases)."

IMPLEMENTATION:

Help children learn to save, *then* spend. Many, perhaps most, impulsive, gotta-have, purchases soon lose their luster. Savvy advertisers are masters at making consumers skip over the 'do I need it', right to the 'I gotta have it' stage. Help a child consider how each possible expense may actually help or hinder his situation in the *long run*.

The excitement of anticipation of possession can be a good part of the saving experience – that's the way I remember it. It took me an entire summer of mowing lawns to buy my J. C. Higgins bicycle when I was ten. You can bet I took good care of it. I do remember the Saturday afternoon dad and I brought it home from Sears and Roebuck. I rode to all my friends' houses and announced, 'See the bike I just bought for myself.' It wasn't just the 'new bike I got' or 'my new bike' – it was 'the bike I bought for myself'. It made me a 'somebody' in my estimation, and in the end, who else's appraisal ever *really* matters? That feeling became an important part of the endeavor – saving necessarily provided that good feeling – that feeling of self-satisfaction and self-confidence if not smug, superiority.

Through the years, I counselled many children who spoke their minds in hurtful ways or lashed out in other inappropriate ways. I had them recreate those situations by building backward from the unpleasant outcome – hurt feelings, loss of a friend, a fight – to craft more helpful reactions – impulse control – a form of delaying the impulsive response to become one more thoughtfully constructed. "What if you had said ___ instead?" "What if you had ignored what she said?" "What if you had decided to think things over and then later offer your response?" "What other more thoughtful ways could you have reacted that would have kept you out of trouble?" Corny as it may seem, I often invoked the, *count to ten*, dictum. Delaying the always destructive expression of hurtful words or anger until your cooler, more thoughtful head can prevail is almost always the more fitting – useful – way to approach human response.

Folks who have learned to curb their impulsive tendencies typically not only have a more satisfying financial life, but also have a higher quality social life than those who have not.

CONCLUSION:

Discounting *that* 'once in a thousand' impulsive stock transaction that worked in one's favor, impulsive behavior is typically a destructive approach to living. Punch the lights out of all the guys who offend you, and your life cannot be comfortable. Make snap decisions without giving adequate thought to their long-term effects, and life cannot be comfortable. The impulsive parent who screams at or hits her child before she has taken time to gather the facts, does the child and the family a great disservice. It is reported that President Nixon, in a drunken, impulsive, stupor decided to bomb Russia. Fortunately, saner minds were present and protected the world from that. When a child establishes and carries with him the gratifying feeling of buying the bike himself, he is well on his way to understanding the up-side of saving now and obtaining later. It also polishes his self-concept, doesn't it?

Think about a world in which nobody could delay personal gratification. Not a pretty picture – a picture clearly suggesting the destruction of mankind.

*****

VALUE PAIR SEVEN:
Helpful
rather than
Hurtful
(includes ignoring)

ILLUSTRATION

As a fourth grader, my son brought a friend home from school.

"This is Joey. He can't read. He does okay with the flashcards I made him with large letters, but it all falls apart when he looks at a page. I told him you could fix him."

It was not the first-time similar events had transpired between that bright, compassionate youngster and his psychologist father.

I asked the boy why he thought he couldn't read.

"Nobody never asked me before. The words fly all over the page."

He had diagnosed his problem, but nobody had ever asked. Grrr! As a psychologist, the first thing I always did was ask the youngster for *his* evaluation of his deficient skill or troublesome situation. They almost always knew.

Watching him try to read, I determined it was his eyes, and not the words, that flew all over the place. I created what would become known as a slot card – it basically directed his vision to one word at a time as he moved the card across a printed line. He read every word with ease, asking what commas and periods were as if he had just discovered them. At the end of the page, all three of us had wet cheeks. I really miss those days.

My son was one of the most altruistic youngsters I have ever known. He had an indomitable sense of justice. He

51

understood his friend's pain was something that could not be tolerated. It was clear he hurt for the boy when, at his success, he shamelessly shed tears of joy. He seldom raised 'easy' challenges for me – never ones I could ignore. Kids are wonderful, the way they force us to grow. (Did I mention that boy had beaten the bejeebies out of my son two weeks prior to this encounter?)

DISCUSSION:

Of all the sets of values, the results of this set may be the most self-evident – helpful vs hurtful. A world populated by helpful folks, empathetic folks, caring folks, has to be superior to one populated by hurtful folks, uncaring folks, selfish folks. *Kindness*, of all the Positive Social Values, may be the most important. Fortunately, it is among the easiest to support and model for our children. "It was so nice to see you helping old Mrs. Stephens with her groceries this morning." "You were so patient with your little brother yesterday when he wasn't feeling good." "Your dad and I hope you will help us deliver Christmas boxes to the old folks tomorrow evening. They all like you so much it will be like an extra present for them to have you there." "Can you arrange to go to Billy's after school? This is my afternoon to help out at the hospital." "The librarian at your school dropped off some old books so we can retape their spines and get them back on the shelves for the kids. She said you are one of her best helpers."

HeCK – **he**lpfulness, **c**ompassion, **k**indness – perhaps the big three of Positive Social Values.

IMPLEMENTATION:

Use the positive value words often with children to keep the concepts alive and active in your home. "Wasn't that *kind* of Mr. Marks to help us fix our screen door?" "I meant to thank you for how *helpful* you were when my friends came for coffee this morning." "You have such a *good heart* – I'm always so proud of how *kind* you are."

Alternatively: "Why do you suppose Mikey always seems to be hurting the other kids?" "I heard Jack and Carl got picked up by the police for vandalizing the school. How do you suppose they came to do such a thing? Your mother and I are so glad we don't have to worry about you ever doing something like that."

CONCLUSION:

Families that use or condone violence, tend to produce children that are v-----t. Families that model kindness and helpfulness tend to produce children that are k--- and h------.

Can you imagine a world filled with hurtful people surviving for very long – certainly not as a safe and comfortable place in which to live and raise children. Can you imagine a world in which children have to be afraid for their safety while they walk from home to school? Oh! Wait!

Hurtfulness tends to initiate hurtfulness in return – you hurt me and I will have to defend myself and my people. Kindness typically does the opposite. This does not deny that there are evil people in the world who will continue to be evil despite the efforts of others to be kind to them. [In my novel, *Envisaging an Ideal Society*, I demonstrate humane methods for dealing with such incorrigibles.   Amazon ISBN 978-1549920523]

When I work with Junior High age youngsters, I simplify the contents of this book by proposing there are three basic ways people approach living.

(1) The Observers – they sit on the sidelines of life neither really trying to make things better for mankind nor trying to hurt it. Not trying to help is, of course, a way of making things worse.

(2) The Destroyers – completely selfish, they take what they want regardless of the damage it does to mankind. Their recklessness and lack of regard for the human species gradually makes life worse for everybody.

(3) The Builders – they believe human life is of highest value, so they work to make life good and preserve Humanity as a happy, content, safe, productive, peaceful species.

That's it. You can only be *one* kind. Pick your role and get to work. Perhaps that is really all that needs to be said.

* * * * *

VALUE PAIR EIGHT
Taking responsibility
rather than
blaming

ILLUSTRATION:

My son entered the kitchen after school – he was twelve. I was there. He put his books on the table and took a seat. He hitched his head for me to join him. Clearly, there was a problem. I sat and waited.

"I did something bad and I don't know how to fix it. It's a lose/lose situation for me. If I fix it, I'll lose three of my friends. If I don't fix it, I'll get a kid in trouble that doesn't deserve it."

"Sounds serious."

"Let me tell you what happened. Five of us were walking home from school like we do most days – we all live down this way – you know the boys. Jerry needed to buy stamps for his mom, so we all went into the post office. While he did what he needed at the counter, the rest of us goofed off – a little chasing and a little shoving. We broke the hinge on one of the glass front doors.

"One of the employees noticed and stood us all up against the wall. Jerry had just rejoined us. The employee accused us of doing the damage. Willy said Jerry had done it and the others nodded to support him. I didn't nod or say anything. I just kept quiet. The employee took Jerry into the office to call his mother. The rest of us left.

"Two things as I see it: One, Jerry and his mother are poor – they can't afford to get the door fixed, and, they shouldn't have to. Two, I just stood there not wanting to get in trouble but not doing anything to defend Jerry. I feel awful. I want to call Jerry, but I have nothing useful to say – 'Sorry, buddy, but at the moment you seemed dispensable'. He's not a close friend, but I don't want him to be in trouble for something the rest of us did."

I tried to help him sort things out. He knew what to do, he just needed the time to bring it into words.

"What's the first thing, the simplest thing for you to do?"

"I need to apologize to Jerry. I need to go over and do it in person – and apologize to his mother, too."

"I agree that's the place to start."

"Yeah, *start*. That means there's one really big thing left to do – go down and talk to the Postmaster. I know that Elmer is one of your friends. I feel bad about that part of it."

"Go on. There's more."

"I don't want to go on, but I know I have to. Will you help me?"

"I'll go with you, of course, but the problems are yours to confront and handle."

He nodded.

"Jerry first and then Elmer, okay?"

"Sounds fine. Want your snack first?"

He shook his head. He wanted to get things handled. That was one of his many admirable qualities.

"It will cost something to get the door fixed. It doesn't seem fair I should have to pay all of it."

"I guess that adds a fourth part to the situation," I said.

"Four?"

"Apologize to Jerry, explain to Elmer, offer to pay your share, and find a way to get the other boys to chip in."

"I really messed up. I'm sorry, dad."

"Two things. Clearly you didn't set out to damage the door – poor judgment is responsible for that – there is a lesson to be learned there – already learned, I'm thinking. Second, you have decided to handle it properly. For that, I'm proud of you. I just imagine you will come up with some ingenious way to get the other boys involved in the payment."

He tried for a smile but settled for a nod.

"Ready? I'll drive us."

"I need to get my money – savings in a shoebox in my dresser."

I remained in the car while he made things right with Jerry and his mother. It proved to be a better relationship than he thought. There was positive spill-over in my direction: a peanut butter cookie and waves and smiles from Jerry and his mom.

At the post office, I stuck my head into Elmer's office.

"Got a boy who wants to speak with you if you have time. I'll wait out here."

My son entered but left the door cracked a bit – his lifeline, I figured. I could hear bits and pieces – two very good people handling a problem calmly and with good sense between them. A few minutes later they emerged from the office.

"Good to see you, Tom. Coffee at the *Busy Bee* in the morning?"

"Sounds good. Seven-thirty!"

Nothing was said about their discussion. Elmer returned inside. The boy beside me sighed and managed a modest smile up into my face. He had just faced and handled the biggest problem of his life to date.

"Elmer's a nice man – a good man. I had enough to cover the cost. I know how I'm going to handle the other boys."

He had things to do, so we parted ways until supper where he emptied pockets of stray bills and coins onto the table.

"I got us all together and we worked it out. I told them I knew that after thinking about it, they were all sorry about how we treated our friend, Jerry. I asked them what we needed to do. They knew. They'll go and talk with Jerry and his mother this evening. After school tomorrow, they'll stop in and talk with Elmer."

He counted the money.

"A dollar too much – like a handling fee, I figure."

We exchanged smiles.

"After supper I'll treat the two best parents in the world to a small swirl at the Dairy Queen."

[Note: during his *teen* years he did NOT always express that same opinion of his progenitors.]

We had a swirl, we had a good talk – it seems we were proud of each other – how nice.

DISCUSSION:

First, neither he nor his father always acted in such mature manners. Mostly, though, things were fine between us and from an early age he was dependably responsible for his years. A sense of responsibility is dependent on several other qualities. One needs to value other people and their right to a good life, before being responsible toward others makes any sense. "His life is as valuable as my life." A *responsible* person (child) is respected and trusted by others – a trait that repays and reinforces itself over and over. That is easily translated onto the international stage. I will let the reader mull that over.

IMPLEMENTATION:
Human beings tend to repeat traits that work and are in other ways rewarded, and they slough off traits that don't work and are seldom or never rewarded. (They move toward the right end of the cubbyholes of the Deep Mind hierarchy of behavioral tendencies.) Families need to help children understand what the good outcomes of relationships are and what the poor outcomes are. Happiness, comfort, harmony, mutual benefits are among the outcomes children must come to seek and demonstrate and prize. It serves them well when there are regular opportunities for a child to demonstrate those things (and find the rewards of doing that). Early on in their lives, they need to have such positive achievements pointed out to them. Eventually, the process becomes self-fulfilling – 'when I help things go better, things are not only better for others but for me as well'. Set up a household that makes people miserable, and its members will be miserable, perpetuating the discomfort. Set it up so it makes people happy and content and self-confident and responsible and mutually helpful, and the family will have a smoother flowing environment and better adjusted people. Well-adjusted folks are always easier to live with than maladjusted. It behooves us to help those around us function in mentally healthy manners. Any idiot can make others miserable. Thoughtful people can make others happy and add to their good adjustment.

Here's a 'thesis' I used to pose to teenagers who were experiencing family problems. "It doesn't matter whether you really want to help members of your family be happier or you just want to make life easier for yourself – don't rock the boat and be a responsible person, and life in your home will improve *for you* like you won't believe." We would talk about how to do that and it actually took less effort than keeping things in an uproar. He – almost always the doubting Thomas – would agree to try it for one week. He was always surprised, shocked, amazed, flabbergasted, astonished, dumbfounded, relieved (and, happier!) . . . [One of my books for teens discusses and demonstrates the process in detail: *How to put up with parents*. It may be out of print, but it is still available on the web.]

CONCLUSION:

It is difficult to teach a child to take responsibility for his actions if he knows he's going to get punished if some misdeed is discovered. Irresponsibility can most effectively be overcome if it is approached as a learning opportunity. What went wrong and what changes would have made it go right? It must become a mental rule that *he* owns, so it becomes his guide wherever he is. Remember, such *portable*, self-imposed rules are called *values*.

Instead of learning he is bad or needs to lie to avoid punishment, the child learns useful methods and grows a positive sense of self-worth as he learns he has the power to face things and fix things – even better, to prevent unpleasant things. Everybody errs sometimes. *Face it and fix it fast*, needs to become the automatic response. Kids who know they can bank on support rather than disparagement or punishment, have the best chance of righting things for all concerned. Rather than pronouncing dictums, we help the youngster discover helpful approaches, don't we? I suppose that is the secret to good parenting regardless of what aspect we might be talking about, isn't it? Lessons that emerge from within a person will last a lifetime. Lessons 'imposed' from without, typically dissipate soon after the 'teacher' is out of sight. (Imposed as contrasted with taught or modeled.)

Consider a world in which blaming others is the basic approach to working through instances where personal responsibility is on the line. Blaming, of course is a kind of lie. It is, perhaps, worse than disseminating lies because blaming always has as its goal, unfairly destroying someone else to protect oneself. It provides no avenue for either self-improvement or improved relations.

(Sadly, *blame* often becomes the engine that moves politics. Conceive of a politics in which the electorate declares there will be no votes cast for candidates who use the 'blame game'.)

* * * * *

VALUE PAIR NINE:
Reverence and respect for life
rather than
disregard for life

ILLUSTRATION:

It was the summer I was thirteen, recently moved away from all my friends and living, relatively isolated, on a farm for the first time. On a romp through the meadow just down the hill and across the road from our house, at the base of a tall oak tree, I came upon three, naked, baby birds. The nest was nearby, clearly having been dislodged from its place in the branches above by the wind storm the night before. I was moved to reunite them with their nest and set it close to the base of the tree in a naturally sheltered pocket in among the roots.

Having done what I figured I could, I moved on. The further I away I got from them, the more their plight bothered me – helpless little beings I had left to die.

Suddenly, saving their lives seemed like the right thing to do. I returned and picked up the nest. At my presence, their large mouths opened, and they made noises more typical of beings four times their size. That cinched it – they were depending on me.

I took them up the hill to the house and I did what I could to make them comfortable in an open cigar box lined with rags. I set it on the floor close to the water heater to provide warmth. I swatted flies and dug worms for three days. It was never enough. They screamed all day. They screamed all night. Regardless of my best efforts, one by one they closed their eyes and no longer spread their beaks when I approached them. I buried them, then went to my room and cried into my pillow for a long time. I couldn't be sure if that were because I was sad for their loss or disturbed by the revelation that I could not fix everything that needed fixing in the world. I still weep over the fate of those babies; I still weep

61

over the revelation.

DISCUSSION:

In 1942, when I was four, and I first came to understand that, in war, groups of men killed each other, I was deeply saddened. My young stomach carried a knot for weeks. A year or so ago, while I was writing the antiwar novel, *Jonathon Penny: his search for life's truths,* the knot returned as it has periodically throughout my life – truthfully, I suppose, it has never had a chance to leave. During my lifetime, our young soldiers have continually been killing somebody else's young soldiers and have been being killed by them. Our legal system has been killing wrong doers. Boys in the alleys of the poor sections of our cities have been killing each other. Shooters have been killing students in our schools and workers in workplaces. The blockbusters of cinema thoughtlessly kill folks off as if they were mosquitos on a bug zapper on the patio on a summer evening. Life has not been revered.

The world I have lived in has *not* modeled that human life is dear. It has trivialized it. In my home, life was sacred. Most of the young men from the church I was raised in became conscientious objectors during WWII, Vietnam, and Korea. They served as noncombatants. Initially, I registered that way but later changed my position and agreed to serve as a battlefield medic in order to save lives. I understand the need to protect one's self and those dear to me and that there can be no black and white about it. To kill or not to kill is perhaps the most terrible quandary of life for those of us who respect and revere it.

IMPLEMENTATION:

During a child's early years, I suppose we begin by modeling reverence and respect for life at the other end of the animal chain – insects – then wild animals, pets and family members. Inspect the tiniest creatures with a magnifying glass, learn their names, look up what they eat and what sort of environment they need in order to flourish. Do they provide anything useful in their relationship with humans? Bees are a wonderful starting place – hurtful to helpful – that is always the secret to an improved perspective – ant or aunt. Set up a 'dinner table' for ants – overly ripe fruit and vegetables, a few sprinkles of ground beef. Plant and care for a 'Bee Bistro' with a variety of plants – tall and short in a variety of colors and blossoms. A young caretaker of nature is soon well on her or his way to understanding the sanctity of life.

Take our children to visit old people and sick people. Chat; maybe take bouquets or handmade do-dads. Request pictures together. Encourage them to tell about how it was when they were growing up. Help them feel important even in their old age and appreciated for how they lived good and helpful lives early on. Those exercises move well beyond improving the lives of the old folks. The more important lesson: Folks who help each other, come to respect and value each other. Folks who help each other, don't kill each other.

At five, I marched into the Mayor's office and told him to have the army boys send their guns to my Dad and he'd take care of them. That way the war would stop. (I was into Saving Humanity from an early age, you see!)

CONCLUSION:

If one wanted to create a society that would most certainly destroy itself, first, one would foster distrust, and then one would model well to the children that extreme punishment, maiming, and killing are all appropriate ways in which to handle conflict, and that meanness, fighting, revenge, and disrespect are proper, if not essential, to protecting oneself. Teach the children they must arm themselves to survive the dangerous world. Doing these things will surely send the world into a downward spiral toward quick oblivion.

Model trust, the value of life, and openness, acceptance, education, and positive problem-solving techniques – that's how we meet conflicts and misunderstandings in a world based in reverence and respect for life.

[Value pair nine is closely tied to value group ten, just below.]

Jonathan Penny: his search for life's elusive truths, by Tom Gnagey, 2020, Amazon 979-8670202107

* * * * *

VALUE PAIR TEN:
Altruism (looking out for others)
rather than
Selfish (mostly just looking out for oneself)

ILLUSTRATION 'A':

I grew up in the 1940s and 50s in a home that was Republican politically (low taxes, small government, privacy) but Democratic socially (government should do what was needed for social safety nets and, personally, we should make certain that nobody within our reach wanted for what they needed or deserved). In the small communities in which I lived, that combination worked very well because neighbors just naturally took good care of neighbors, so government was not compelled to assume much of that role. There were a few greedy people in my life back then, but by and large we were altruistic and compassionate types eager to make the positive difference. My family often, and with no remorse, did without so folks in more need got what they required. It is my well-ingrained approach to life to this day and I treasure and highly recommend it. Those of us who have more (even just a little more), have the grand privilege of assisting those who have too little. Life, not stuff is sacred.

A more specific example: After each winter snow (I grew up in northern Illinois), the kids in my town got up early and shoveled the walks and driveways for the old folks and others we figured couldn't do it themselves. My 'team' of four buddies from the neighborhood ended such sessions in my kitchen, telling our tales of the morning over hot buttered toast and hot chocolate (always called *cocoa*, in those days). The more we talked, the better we felt about ourselves. By the time we arrived at school (there were never snow days) we were overflowing with feelings of self-worth and I'm sure 'it' overflowed into a good day in the classroom.

65

[Charging or accepting money for the shoveling was unthinkable – disgusting, and belittling, in fact! The idea of profiting from someone's misfortune was a fully unfathomable concept to us as I'm sure it is for the reader.]

ILLUSTRATION 'B':

It was December of 1943 or 1944, I imagine. There was a Japanese internment camp just up the road from the little town in northern Illinois where I lived as a six- or seven-year-old. Before the cold weather set in, I had stood out front and watched the open trucks filled with Japanese families move north along the road in front of my house. I had waved to the children. They had waved back.

When daddy said grace one evening – close to Christmas – he asked that the Japanese families be warm and that their Christmases be good.

My bike and I had clandestinely visited the camp on several occasions, and I had talked through the wire fence to one of the boys – about my age – a bit younger. I always tried to raise his spirits – a trait I learned early from my family. Anyway, I told a fib to mother – that I was going over to play with Jerry. Instead, I gathered all my presents from under the tree – five as I recall, they fit into a brown paper bag from the grocery store – and I headed off through the fallen snow to the camp. Kim's family's tent was close to an area of the fence seldom visited by the guards and I found him easily. (A determined six-year-old can get most anywhere he wants, any time he wants to.) The sack was too big to fit through the wire so, after several attempts, I managed a toss that sent it over the top. We laughed about my several failures.

As he examined the contents, he spread a smile such as I've never seen. He reached into his pocket and pulled out a large, red button and slipped it to me through the wire. I understood it was for some reason precious to him. We said thank you and wished each other a merry Christmas.

Please understand, this is NOT a tribute to me – it is a tribute to my parents who, to this day, continue to be my most cherished models – if only in memory, now.

DISCUSSION:

My parents believed that nobody should have to do without what they needed. They believed it was a basis of the social contract we all agree to when we decide to live with and among others in a group setting. They believed it was an honor to provide one's excess to those in need. If the world had been organized according to *their* beliefs, those who are able to provide the most assistance would be the most honorable among men.

I won't pretend that I have always lived up to their standards, but it has been my goal. The most basic definition of Altruism implies one puts others needs before one's own. Understanding the human psyche, that has never seemed feasible for members of my species. In my mind, altruism has come to mean putting the needs of others at least on a par with one's own. I realize even that is a substantial goal. The question I ask myself is, 'Do I really need that ______ (new pair of shoes) more than the starving children need the food that money could buy them?'

[My college speech teacher said that when a speaker was trying to persuade a person to move his belief an inch, he often needed to ask him to move it a mile. Sad, but clearly true.]

IMPLEMENTATION:

Most parents urge their children to share – a difficult concept for the naturally self-centered youngster (the prime directive, remember – me, me, me!). The urge to share is only clinched when the associated response (feeling) is positive. "Share your book or I'll slap you silly," probably doesn't teach it. "Let me share my cookie with you, son," is undoubtedly the best initial modeling. The old rule about *showing* kids rather than *telling* kids is the surest path to success in establishing all values – negative or positive.

CONCLUSION:

A child learns what he sees and feels. When he is raised in a positive atmosphere, he will most likely acquire those positive, helpful, altruistic values. When he is raised in a 'me first', hoarding, selfish, hurtful, atmosphere, he will most likely acquire those negative, socially harmful values. *THAT part of saving humanity is simple* – no excuses – has been proven without a doubt during centuries of human existence. Kindness begets kindness.

* * * * *

VALUE PAIR ELEVEN:
Accurately informed decision making (facts)
rather than
uninformed or lore-base decision making (ignorance)

ILLUSTRATION:
This could just as well have been set up as *Eager to Learn* rather than *Willing to remain Ignorant.*

As a second grader, I had a heated debate with a classmate. We lived next door to each other and often had heated debates. We were best friends except when we weren't. He insisted blankets gave off heat. I asked him to show me how they did that.

First, he said, "Everybody knows that. There's nothing to show."

I said, 'what everybody knows' is not proof.

"Yes, it is."

"No, it isn't."

 He pulled the blanket around his shoulders and said he felt warmer with it around him.

"You know you feel warmer under a blanket," he continued.

I suggested we put it to a test. We wrapped a wall thermometer in a wool blanket – eight, maybe ten thicknesses. I wrote down the temperature it registered before. He agreed. After ten minutes we unwrapped it. The temperature had not changed. He said the thermometer was 'broke'. I closed my palm around the bulb. The temperature moved up rapidly.

His parting words, "You're stupid."

Little did I realize *that* day that I had just witnessed what would become the paradigm for critical thinking among a vast number of less educated people who I would encounter later as my life lapped over into the 21st century.

DISCUSSION:

Gently require children (and adults) to support answers with facts. If they don't have them, don't fault them, help them find them. Help them learn how to find them if they don't know. The most accurate thinkers ask, 'how' rather than 'why'. Answers to 'why' allow if not encourage opinions or unfounded reasons. 'How' questions (How did you come to believe that, or how could that have come to be) encourage the use of facts.

IMPLICATION:

Urge children to ask questions. Teach them how to ask useful questions. Guide children to find their own answers. Help them learn how to check their answers for accuracy. Remember, it is always better to answer honestly when we don't have an answer. It allows a wonderful triple learning moment – first, 'let's find the answer together', 'find the answer and increase one's fund of knowledge', and third, 'learn it's fun and important to search for answers backed by facts.'

My son, as a fifth grader, proudly offered at supper that his teacher asked the class a question and nobody knew the answer. "Can we find out about it after supper?" In our home, we were eager to learn new things and face new challenges in our home. Ignorance was downright scary. I urge us to always meet, "I don't know," with, "Great, how can we find out?"

CONCLUSION:

Your unfounded lore is never as good as my carefully researched facts. Many folks, today, really and truly do not understand that. There is work to do! A humanity that seeks and reveres facts and fact-based answers has a great chance at survival in comfort, contentment, and the advantages of progress. It is as if a large group of folks are willingly reverting to our caveman heritage when lore, superstition, and correlation were all they had to rely on for explanations, so they let it rule them. They abdicate the use of the human mind. A humanity that becomes satisfied with lore, rumors, and opinion is destined to destroy itself.

* * * * *

VALUE PAIR TWELVE:
Being known by ones good reputation
rather than
trying to be known as a somebody at any cost

* * * * *

ILLUSTRATION:

Sixth grade was the first time we had Class Presidents in my school. Over a period of several days, our teacher spent time talking with us about leadership traits and good reputations and such. A local preacher gave a five-minute talk about goodness (it was 1949, remember): it lasted a half hour and was sprinkled with church words like wrath, sin, and hell. Later, the teacher gave us an opportunity to ask questions of her. She had determined three students could be nominated for President and asked us to discuss the topic among ourselves. The following morning, each of the nominees was to give a five-minute talk about why they should be elected, and the voting would be done by secret ballot at the end of the day. All that seemed reasonable – as an eleven-year-old, I knew the basics of democracy.

Much to my surprise, I was nominated. That possibility had not entered my head. I kept it to myself at home and spent the evening in my room working on a speech. The basic premise bothered me – 'Why I wanted to be president'. I hadn't wanted to be president – Mary Lou wanted me to be president – she had nominated me. The following morning, we drew straws to fix the order for our speeches. I was last. I figured that was good. I listened to the others. They were filled with promises that could *not* be fulfilled – two sloppy Joes each at lunch, hamburgers twice a week, extended recesses, no more Friday test days, and so on.

I had my turn and talked about having us be kind to each other and help the struggling students study and bringing items for a food shelf so kids from families who needed it could get it – secretly. All things that were important in my home.

The vote would come just before dismissal that afternoon. That meant there were three free times for campaigning before the vote – two recesses and noon hour. Ronnie, the rich kid who had been nominated, spent that time handing out dimes to kids who promised to vote for him. (His mother had delivered several rolls to him at morning recess. Unbelievable!) Butch, the class bully – nominated by his favorite target for reasons of survival – spent the time threatening the kids with what would happen to them if he wasn't elected. I figured I had already had my time to make my pitch so engaged in my usual activity with most of the other guys – a friendly little game with a ball we called, 'Kill the guy that's got it'. (When my son was in sixth grade the game was the same but the name had changed – Throw up and slaughter.)

I knew what the other nominees were up to but didn't express my disapproval as we stood in line at the water fountain.

The teacher had prepared ballots on that purple copy machine in the office. I loved that aroma! The instruction was to put an X in the square beside our choice. I wondered if I should vote for myself. I decided I was the best choice so placed my X. We folded our ballots and handed them forward to the teacher. She picked a boy and a girl to count them. They whispered the result to her and returned to their seats. There were 22 in my class.

The teacher printed the three names on the black board and added the number of votes we each had received.

Ronnie – 1

Butch – 2

Tommy – 19

Nobody seemed savvy enough to understand those figures indicated I had probably voted for myself. I was relieved.

Then, the most useful part of the election happened – perhaps the real purpose for it. The teacher had us discuss why we had each voted like we had. It became a spirited series of good vs evil rants. Catharsis[2]. Even at age eleven, my classmates understood skullduggery when they saw it and how it should be treated. (I didn't notice anybody giving back dimes, however.)

"How did school go today, Tommy?" mother asked as I

walked in the door.

"Okay. I kept the ball in *Kill the guy that's got* it the whole recess this afternoon."

Budding, masculine, self-esteem – 1. Political ambitions – 0.

DISCUSSION:

I was proud of my good reputation. I had known that most of my life. I surely didn't need an election to prove it. It was no secret to me that my family cherished a good reputation. I knew I could count on them to guide me back on the path when I veered. I figured it was a two-way deal: being a good and dependable person helped one gain a good reputation. Protecting one's good reputation required one to continue being a good and dependable person. Another one of those really simple, priceless, aspects of life. (Grampa may have pointed it out to me.)

Ronnie and Butch had missed the point. Ronnie played the rich kid that he figured made him a somebody and somebody's, of course, should receive privileges. Butch played the tough guy. He confused being feared with being respected. Not news to the reader, I'm sure, Ronnie's dad played the rich guy card often – paid for a small chapel on the new Methodist church on the condition it bore his name. Butch's father had been in and out of trouble all his life. Kids learn what they see and experience, don't they.

IMPLEMENTATION:

Implementing the importance of a good reputation is a piece of cake for parents who have established themselves with good reputations. It is what the child sees, lives with, and therefore learns. It also provides a happy and productive tie-in with reading about admirable people. A book that influenced me as a fourth grader was titled: William Penn, friendly boy. Probably corny, but potent. One scene remains with me: *'Seeing the boy with no shoes, William removed his and handed them to his new friend.'*

[I have spent a good part of my life writing novels – many of them for kids and teens – in which the characters model positive social values.]

As adults, we have the obligation and privilege of voting the 'puffed-up guys' out of office, avoiding their businesses, refusing to listen to their hurtful rhetoric, providing information to counter their false or misleading statements. The world needs unity or at least the willingness to work through disagreements in philosophy and policy. Folks who spend their time proving how great they are, are seldom those who work for bettering the human condition. If they can't get credit for it or if things can't have their names attached to them, the 'puffed-up guys', aren't interested. When building one's brand is more important than fostering the general welfare, a man automatically contributes to the destructive, downward spiral of humanity.

CONCLUSION:

Often, of course, people who live their lives promoting themselves in order to be known as *a somebody* are those who have no basic, system of positive core values – no genuine connection with the rest of humanity. They live their lives at a selfish, hollow, level. That defines them as so self-centered (egomaniacal) they cannot understand about the necessary responsibility men must feel toward each other. Such a careless disconnect can only contribute to the death of our species.

* * * * *

VALUE PAIR THIRTEEN:
Kind-hearted
rather than
inconsiderate or otherwise hurtful

ILLUSTRATION:

This story could fit equally well as an illustration for several sets of values. I have concluded this is a good spot. As a 'cub reporter' at a small radio station in the upper Midwest, I had interviewed several celebrities with a variety of pedigrees. I found most of them irritating if not disgusting. Then came this one.

My freshman year in college, I worked at the radio station – WMIB, in North Manchester, Indiana. Eleanor Roosevelt came to speak at my college. The station reporter got sick and I was dispatched to do the interview. Twenty minutes later I realized it had been I who had just been interviewed. Seldom had I felt so important to anybody. She agreed that Socrates was the best name for a family cat she had ever heard. I mentioned he snored. She became all confidential and admitted that so had her husband. She wanted to know the name of the song in which I had a trombone solo when I played in the All-State band my junior year in high school. She asked what I looked for in a new friend. In the end, she told me what an honor it had been for her to have been interviewed by me. What a magnificent human being she was. My story reflected what she had helped me learn about myself and certain personal characteristics I found myself striving for. It won me a Collegiate Journalism Award that year. I sent her a copy of the article and the award. [Mrs. Roosevelt, White House, Washington, D.C.] She responded. "I remember, Tommy. You wore a black and gold Beta Club pin – the first time I learned about that honor society. I know you are going to have a fine life."

A second Illustration from my journal:

I woke up this morning with the vision of a seven- or eight-year-old boy who I met early during the 9 or so months my life took a frightening turn and I had to live as a street person. I was sitting on cement steps apparently not hiding very well that I was a newcomer to the homeless life.   He came up and sat beside me. He handed me an empty cereal box.

"Thanks, but I don't understand."

He removed one of his shoes and pointed inside.

"You can cut insoles to cover the holes in your shoes, so the sidewalks don't cut your feet."

He smiled up at me. He patted me on my knee and left. I never saw him again.

Thanks 'Smiling Cereal Box Boy". No one has ever made a kinder or more compassionate gesture to me.

One more illustration about kindness:

On my walk this morning, I came upon a boy – maybe eight – sitting on the sidewalk holding a puppy.

"What a cute puppy. Is he yours?"

"No, but he's my best friend."

"I see. He sure seems to like you."

"He likes me mostly when I have food for him."

"Oh?"

"Yeah. I know *I'm* not *his* best friend, but that's okay."

"So, you feed him."

"Yeah. So does Mrs. Walker and Grampa James on the corner."

He pointed down the street.

"He gets real dog food from them. I only got bread and some mornings left-over oatmeal."

"Pup is lucky to have such good friends. Does he not have a home?"

"Don't seem to. When I leave, he disappears. That don't mean he got a home. Might just mean he's scared, you know."

"Have you thought about asking your folks if you can keep him?"

"Pup don't want to be mine. He likes Mrs. Walker and Grampa James, too. Wouldn't be fair if I took them away from him."

"You seem to understand things pretty well."

"Me and him is a lot alike. He's like a foster pup and I'm a foster kid. It's never easy to get pulled away from folks you like and be sat down with new ones."

"Well, I'm sure it must be great for him to have a kind and thoughtful boy like you in his life right now."

He nodded.

"I know."

He pulled the pup close, cheek to cheek. I said my good-bye and walked on. The two of them had worked out a good thing between them. The boy understood that. He knew it was a short-term arrangement. His well-learned lessons from life were to hold no long-term expectations and do whatever it took to make the best of every moment – kindness with no consideration of personal advantage.

Sadly, all I had for him was the tear that made its way down my face and got lost in my scraggly, old, gray, chin whiskers.

DISCUSSION:

This was a kindhearted youngster – who knew why? Perhaps because he understood the importance of having kindhearted people in *his* life. 'I will do what I can for the people who come into my life because that's how life should be.' He asked nothing from the puppy other than to let him love it and provide what good care he could. Some youngsters in his place would have felt jealous of the puppy – getting the care and attention of Mrs. Walker and Grampa James. Such feelings easily translate to the need to punish – mistreat. He made no attempts at establishing a relationship with me – one more person to lose. That may have included *him* losing me and *me* losing him – a way of avoiding sadness for both of us. He wasn't about to give puppy a false sense of security by taking him on as his own or taking him away from the adults he understood were in a better position to care for him.

We should all have friends like 'Pup Boy' and 'Cereal Box Boy'. We should all *be* friends like 'Pup Boy' and 'Cereal Box boy'. I just imagine most of us are. Few, if any, of us will ever be an Eleanor Roosevelt but that doesn't mean we can't reflect her grace, compassion and perceptive outreach.

IMPLEMENTATION:

I remember an important conversation when I was six or seven. I had had a "fight" with my friend Jimmy who lived across the street. My mother asked what happened.

"I'm not sure. I was helping him get their fishing poles ready for Saturday – they are going to their shack at the river. I had never done it before and made a mistake and he raised a pole up and hit me with it across my arms."

"Are you okay?"

"I am, but Jimmy isn't. He can't keep popping off like that. Soon he won't have any friends at all. I may even give up on him."

"Any idea why he does that – pop off?"

"Sure. His dad does it to him all the time."

There was no doubt in my mind about 'why he did it' – how he had come about the reaction. Even at such a young age, children understand about the importance of modeling – acting toward others the way parents act toward them. After all, they have looked to the grownups their entire lives for how to do all the grownup stuff they don't yet know how to do.

I worked with many neglected children ten and under in my years of association with the Department of Child and Family Services. I would often ask them what one thing they were going to make sure they did with their children every day. Dependably, their faces lit up and they talked on and on about whatever it was. It almost always pointed me in the direction of some underlying malady and the remedial actions we needed to implement. Kids are so smart if we just listen.

CONCLUSION:

Kindhearted can have a number of opposites depending on situations: hurting, punishing, disregarding, cruelty, hateful, heartless, rejection. It is impossible to see how any of those can contribute to an improved human condition or planet on which to live. The regular demonstration of any one of them can immediately become a force against our survival. They are incompatible alternatives to kindness – incompatible in that the two cannot be simultaneously exhibited. One has to wonder how so many people grow up without adequate modeling of kindheartedness – one of those things we all seek or at least hope for. I had a sociology professor who said: "If it weren't for kindness, there could be no human race."

* * * * *

VALUE PAIR FOURTEEN:
Try to understand others who are different rather than
Ignore, exclude, or hurt them.

ILLUSTRATION: [After one of my Winter Holiday short stories]

It was a cold, December evening. The light, but constant, snowfall of the afternoon had moderated to flurries with the setting sun. Old Jake was trudging the alley that took him from the grocery store to the place he lived – a small, two-story, older house crunched between two, taller, newer, business buildings. The moon was large and brightened the world as it sparkled the smooth, new, moist, fallen snow.

There were boot prints ahead of him – clearly those of a youngster – heading east like he was. Presently he saw the boy to whom the boots were attached. He was digging through the snow to find stones – stones he was throwing at an upstairs window on Jake's house.

The old man moved toward the boy to determine what was going on and why.

Crash! The window was broken.

The boy turned around and hurried right into Jake's waiting arms.

"I believe I need an explanation. That is my window you just broke."

The boy looked terrified. He had no words.

"Tell me this, son. If somebody broke the window in your room, don't you think you would deserve an explanation – the who and why of it?"

"I guess."

"Do you think I need to talk with your parents about this or do you think you and I can work something out just between the two of us?"

"Just the two of us sounds good."

"It's cold and you are shivering. Come inside with me and we can discuss things further over buttered toast and mugs of hot chocolate."

"What?"

"Did I not speak loud enough? Sometimes I don't. I'm hard of hearing."

"I heard."

The old man pointed to the gate and the narrow walk that led to the back porch.

"Please stomp your feet before entering."

He did. Jake opened the door, reached inside, and turned on the kitchen light. He ushered the boy in ahead of him and closed the door behind them.

"Hooks there to hang your cap and jacket. You know how to make hot chocolate?"

"I've watched ma make it."

"I bet you can do it then. After you remove your boots, fill the tea kettle with hot water, put it on the small burner and turn the flame up high. I'll get the cocoa and bread."

Jake sat at the table and removed his boots. The boy followed the directions, yet he clearly remained puzzled.

They were soon sitting across the small, round, table from each other sipping and munching.

"Excellent toast, son. You must have had practice."

There was no response to the comment. There were words, however.

"What's going on here, Old Man?"

"How rude of me. My name is Jake, however, it doesn't bother me to be called Old Man. You're Scotty Atherton, aren't you?"

"How you know that?"

"I've lived here twenty years – twice as long as you've been alive."

"So?"

"So, I figured it would be good to be on a first name basis before we go upstairs so you can fix my broken window."

"I don't know how to fix a broken window."

"Fortunately, I do. I will instruct you."

"I don't get you."

"And I don't get you but that doesn't make us even. You still owe me the repair of one windowpane."

They finished at the table and proceeded up the stairs to the storeroom at the rear.

"You pick up all the glass and put it in that bucket. I'm sure you will be careful, so you don't cut yourself. I have a spare pane and putty in the closet. I'm going to assume this wasn't entirely your idea."

Scotty was happy to buy into that – spread the blame.

"The big guys. Said before I could hang out, I had to prove my loyalty, and this is what I had to do to prove it."

"You thought breaking an old man's window was okay?"

"I knew it wasn't."

After nearly an hour, they had completed the project – patiently, Jake had Scotty do every step with no more assistance than necessary.

"A very nice job, Scotty. You are good at such things."

It garnered a weak smile.

"Your glass is in backwards, Jake. The putty goes on the outside and not on the inside like here. Why this way?"

"For many years now, the older guys have had the younger guys break my window. So, I fixed it to make it easy on myself."

"That's awful."

It had slipped out before Scotty recognized what he was saying.

"I'll pay for it. Don't know how, but I will. I really am sorry."

"How about we make a deal?"

"A deal?"

"The bill for the material is nine dollars. You will come and spend an hour with me every Saturday morning. I'll take a dollar off your bill each time you come."

"I don't get it."

"I know you don't. You will someday. Is it a deal?"

"I guess. The older guys said you were weird and that made it ok for me to break your window. They say you never speak when you pass us on the walk – like you're stuck up – think you're better than us."

"Like I said, I am hard of hearing and with all the outside noise, I don't hear what others might say to me. It is never my intention to ignore anybody."

Silence, then . . .

"I bet you know Kenny White, don't you?"

"What makes you say that?"

"He told me not to do it. He said you were okay."

"Let me put it this way, Scotty; you just might find his fingerprints on that old putty you just removed."

DISCUSSION:

It takes us back to the discussion about one of the basic, Deep Mind, tenets; if you can't be sure some other person is completely safe, consider them unsafe and find ways of keeping your distance. Ignoring them, excluding them, and hurting them, are, in increasing order of severity, three ways of accomplishing that. Also, of course, it is always easier to hurt somebody you don't know. None of those can bring folks closer and reduce the perceived threat level. Only getting to know each other in a safe environment has the potential for doing that.

This doesn't imply that doing that will automatically prove you will feel safe with them or that you even like them as people. One might mix with a group of strangers and find he really doesn't like them or can't feel comfortable around them. At least that feeling will have been based in fact, rather than merely in suspicion. It's usually better to gather the facts than it is to proceed according to supposition, lore, rumor, and ignorance.

As most of us have learned, the same goes for general questions: search out the facts rather than accepting unfounded assumption and speculation.

IMPLEMENTATION:

Homes are different in how open they are to new or different things/ideas/people. My wife and I tried to establish the belief in our home that learning new things was wonderful – necessary even for self-fulfillment. We provided books on a variety of topics – a set of encyclopedias – and regularly frequented the library. (An hour or so after my wife gave birth, I was allowed to go see her and my new son in her room – it was the protocol of 1961. I took each of them a book. Did I get looks from the staff! No roses. No candy. Books. They would have been amazed if they had stuck around and listened to him read to us – just kidding – I do that sometimes.)

We always answered questions and pointed our son, and the foster boys who lived with us, in useful directions for more information. We made a point of engaging folks from other cultures. We hosted students studying from abroad. We cared for foster kids who had grown up in subcultures very different from the one we had established for our son. We went for the belief, 'So, he's different. How great. What can we learn from him? What can we share with him?' We offered reasonable safeguards. It didn't always work. Of course, it *never* could have worked had we not tried. (Parenting is a tough job. It requires careful, regular planning and well-taken thoughtfulness, doesn't it?)

CONCLUSION:

In the larger sense, a peaceful, mutually helpful world, cannot exist when there is an undercurrent of distrust and ignorance of the ways and beliefs of 'those others'. Common ground cannot be established if we don't understand each other's 'ground' – beliefs, capacities, knowledge, hopes, fears, needs, goals, and so on. Attempts at understanding and reconciliation will fail without that careful search for common threads.

In less dire and more informal settings, the full story may not be necessary. In the building where I live with lots of other old people, there is a wonderful cross section of humanity – colors, ethnicity, educational levels, interests, backgrounds, geographic origins, political proclivities, and teeth or no teeth. We don't need the full resume to treat each other in warm, civil ways, and be supportive when someone is in obvious stress or pain, and to revel with them in their successes and the happy events in their lives. This very morning, I spent several minutes with a near stranger, looking at her new pictures of her grandchildren. She knew I'd be interested. I was. What's better than pictures of children with their pets or birthday cakes? I'm sure the readers regularly have similar experiences. They are more than just happy encounters; they maintain the bond that holds the human species together in positive, trusting, humanity-friendly, humanity-saving ways.

* * * * *

VALUE PAIR FIFTEEN:
Seek to understand Intentions
rather than
Assuming you understand a person's motivation

ILLUSTRATION:

It was Christmas morning the year my son was three. Clearly, my present from my wife was a book. I unwrapped it – a first edition of one of my favorite authors. I opened it and to my surprise the front page had Crayola marks on it – a remnant of some encounter with a child back when, I figured. I turned the page – more Crayola marks – clearly purposeful – just in the margins. In the end, every page had been marked. I understood my son had been busy ruining my book. I *didn't* understand why he would have done that. Was he angry at me? What message was he sending me? What was going on? I showed it to my wife. She wrinkled her brow, as stunned as I was. I turned to Bobby and held out the book, ready to confront him over it. He put on a grin and climbed into my lap, arms around my neck, and kisses to my temple.

"Do you like it, daddy? I made the book beautiful for you."

I paused but a moment. He had clearly spent hours working on it.

"I love it, son. What a wonderful present. You chose my favorite colors and made wonderful designs like I've never ever seen before. Thank you."

I was able to smile, thinking, '*two* first editions'.

It was a wonderful hug I will never forget. It was a grand lesson I hope I never forget.

DISCUSSION:

Discovering intentions – the reasons behind a behavior – is best approached as one of those, '*how* did one come to decide on that approach', questions. '*Why*' typically muddies it up with 'our' idea rather than 'his'.

How does one investigate motive? Being familiar with a person's traits is perhaps the best way – 'what motive makes sense knowing who he is?' In situations that offer negative outcomes, look for a positive intention first. Mistakes and misinterpretations occur, and if the person mistakenly felt threatened, a seemingly out of place reaction may have reasonably taken place.

Perhaps the most definitive method for ascertaining intention is to ask the person or somebody close to him. For young children or people experiencing a mental health emergency, they may consciously have no idea what motivated them to do something. Subconscious motivation is a fascinating field within psychology.

IMPLEMENTATION:

Ten-year-old to his mother:

"He hit me because he hates me."

"Maybe. How would he have come to hate you?"

"I don't know. I've always treated him good."

That is the beginning of a necessary conversation whenever the question of intent arises. It forces a change in direction from baseless accusation to the serious examination of the situation.

To encourage a modified perspective, the conversation might continue in this way:

"How might you come to hit him?"

"If he hit me first."

"But you didn't do that. How else?"

"If I thought he was going to hurt me or if I heard he planned to hurt my friend."

"So, there could be several reasons."

"I guess."

"How can you know for sure, so maybe you can keep it from happening again?"

"You mean, talk to him about it?"

(One might get the idea he'd heard that before.)

The conversation might not go that smoothly, but that's the general plan. The lesson is, 'Don't jump to conclusions; gather the information needed for proper examination. The process is, 'help the youngster (or ourself) learn how to use the 'How' questions rather than the 'Why' questions *or* no questions at all.

CONCLUSION:

We often read our own motives into other people's intentions – we must ask ourselves if that's what we are doing. Since a person's intentions are an outgrowth of how his life experiences are reflected in his response, and since we are typically not privy to those, it behooves us not to rush in applying our own.

In *his* experience, how have situations affected him in the past – interactions with teachers, police, white people, purple people, children, adults, old people, people like you, chameleons – that list goes on?

Bottom line, assumptions about the basis of somebody else's response or behavior, which is based on *our* experiences, are hardly ever going to be correct. Allowing or promoting unnecessary misunderstanding is a sure way to add to the downfall of the human species. There are enough genuine ways in which it comes about – so avoid misinterpretation. It is seldom a good idea to go with your first thoughts – impressions – because they will reflect you not them.

Bottom line: we must not assume we understand another person's intention until we have gathered sufficient data. In a world where first impressions become final impressions, misunderstanding will run rampant. That can't promote a good life. It can easily be seen how it could promote the disintegration of society.

* * * * *

VALUE PAIR SIXTEEN:
Fair treatment and honesty
rather than
deceit and dishonesty

ILLUSTRATION 'A':

I was new to the school. I was a new 8th grader. I was not new to science classes – I had had them since fourth grade. I'll call him Butch – one of several boys who picked me out as a 'damnyankee' to pick on, to put me down, to prove that Arkansas boys were in every way superior to Illinois boys. It was the first time I had encountered really mean, physically abusive boys.

Immediately after the first big exam in science, Butch raised his hand and told the teacher (who really didn't know me from Adam, yet) that I had been copying his answers. I figured from the quick on and off smile she had flashed, she understood. I raised my hand, not in defense, but suggesting a solution.

"When you go over the test with us, now, how about letting me give the answer to each of the questions – just to see if it seems like I might have copied his answers?"

She agreed. She took it one step further. "First, I will read Butch's answer to each question and then Tommy's. I assume you cannot object to that, Butch."

He squirmed and shrugged. He may have slid down just a bit in his seat. There were soft chuckles. Big Butch wasn't used to being challenged.

There were 25 questions; in the end Butch got five of ten true/false questions right and Tommy got all 25 right – 26 if you included my rewrite of her question #9, since it had a faulty assumption that made it invalid.

The teacher's only remark was directed at Butch. "Maybe you should move to the desk *behind* Tommy where you will have a better view of *his* test sheet during the next exam.

Giggles from the girls, boisterous guffaws from the boys, and most important to me, I suppose, Butch never offered his

89

threatening put downs again – well, suddenly going from 'anonymous new guy Tommy' with complexion problems, to the smartest 8th grader wasn't all that bad either.

ILLUSTRATION 'B':

I suppose I was eight. One Saturday morning dad asked me to accompany him – he had some business to take care of. I was eager to get to spend private time with him. It meant combing my hair and brushing my shoes – important, see! He parked in front of the bank and we entered. Mr. Loomis greeted us and ushered us into his office.

Dad stated his reason for being there.

"I need two-hundred and fifty dollars to put toward a new car."

He showed the man the paperwork. It seemed to me dad must have already saved over one thousand dollars toward it. He didn't believe in borrowing money, so I figured it was some sort of emergency. A month later mom had surgery. I figured *that* was the emergency.

"I have my house to offer as collateral. It is paid in full."

"You should know I'd never need collateral from you, Mr. Gnagey. Your word is good enough for me."

The details were worked out and fifteen minutes later we left with a large, greenish colored check.

Once I asked about and received an explanation of the universal use of collateral in such transactions, my hero became my superhero – dad was such a good man even the bank president trusted him. I had watched them shake hands – firm, long and warm – I came to treasure a shake and what it meant – a pledge and its acceptance between men who trusted and respected each other – who were prepared to treat each other fairly and honestly. I had to wonder if Jimmy's dad would have received the same treatment. I figured not. We kids couldn't trust Jimmy – he lied a lot. Like child, like parent, seemed to answer my question.

DISCUSSION:

The idea of habitual deceit and dishonesty hadn't entered my life until, at five, I moved next door to the aforementioned, Jimmy. At the end of the first day, I had a bedtime discussion with dad. "Do you think Jimmy really flies an airplane Sunday mornings instead of going to church."

"That seems unlikely."

"He says his uncle is King of Indiana."

"Impossible."

"He says a lot of stuff that I don't believe. When I tell him I think he's fibbing, he gets really mad. How come he tells lies all the time?"

Now, I had told little fibs from time to time – that I had taken only one cookie from the jar when I had actually taken two – things like that. Protecting myself in that way was not necessary at my house, but sometimes I felt it was good to be prepared, just in case.

Lying is closely tied to trust and trust among men may be the most important deterrent to the collapse of our species. Early experiences with people who lie, quickly teach youngsters that they cannot be trusted. And, once not trusted, never fully trusted again.

Today, the fabrication of inaccurate information – often by the more ignorant (more poorly informed) among us – seems to have become a way of life in many quarters. Some lie to protect themselves from serious repercussions. Some lie to avoid looking uninformed. Some lie to protect their point of view. Some lie to hurt or misdirect others. Regardless of the motivation, the dissemination of false information, destabilizes society, rather than contributing to its strength and stability. A lie coming from a trusted source is the most dangerous and despicable of all.

IMPLICATION:

When a parent lies to a child about one thing, and the child finds out, the child must question whether they can trust *anything* he tells him. Imagine what the inability to trust the most important person in his life means to him – he no longer has a source of truth or right or wrong or proper answers to his important questions. Fear encroaches on most aspects of his life. It, also, gives *him* permission to lie. Acting on that, he loses credibility among his peers and teachers – he must traverse life without the most basic, necessary, positive, interpersonal trait. That means few if any comfortable close friends. It means destabilization of society where he touches it. It probably also translates into failed marriages later in life.

Fair treatment of others begets fair treatment for you.

Deceitful treatment of others begets distrust, dislike, and distance from the positive social union. The verdict is swift and permanent – one lie and you're always suspect – always.

CONCLUSION:

Values have a way of compounding. My father's good reputation (Value 12) coupled with his known honesty made him a spotless credit risk. People admired and trusted him in our little town. Nobody trusted Jimmy, or any member of his family, or any of his close friends. Folks like my dad are the glue that holds society together and offers hope for a positive future. Folks like Jimmy – well . . .

Take a moment and imagine a world in which everybody could trust everybody else on all matters. Imagine a world in which nobody could trust anybody on any matter, whatsoever. We immediately understand which situation will foster the collapse of society and the destruction of the species.

* * * * *

VALUE PAIR SEVENTEEN:
Positive, value-based, openness
rather than
belief in mindless absolute right and wrong

ILLUSTRATION ONE:

An exercise I often used when I taught Adolescent Psychology to college freshmen went like this. I pre-arranged with one of the students to purportedly do something inappropriate in class – plagiarize, cheat on a test, or so on. The class was made aware of it. At the next session I announced that the 'bad boy' had agreed to let the class members discuss his predicament and recommend what the consequences should be. Each conclusion offered had to be backed by the reasons.

Initially, those typically reflected their unexamined beliefs of absolute right and wrong – dad says so, the church says so, I've always believed that, it only seems right that, everybody knows that . . . . If nobody suggested asking the 'bad boy' for his take on it, I would eventually do that. He and I had worked out a story ahead of time – one that moved the motivation from the obvious assumptions to the exceptional and idiosyncratic. It revealed things the group had not considered.

Those things became part of the conversation. In every instance, the absolute positions of right and wrong cracked and the concept of individual differences emerged as a powerful force in the discussion. Not, 'this severe thing should happen to him because he did wrong', but 'considering what we know about the situation, he should be allowed to _______ (make amends and if he needs some sort of assistance, there were always volunteers, etc.).

Most of the students were adolescents – those creatures so often guided by the most absolute of absolutes – clothing choices, hair styles, language choices, importance of social class and associations, friendships, in-groups, out-groups, and on and on – and given to doling out mindless, often hurtful, consequences

93

to their 'wayward' peers. (Remember, the human brain doesn't have 'full logical capacity' and 'mature critical thinking skills' until the early twenties.)

At the following class meeting I asked them to discuss how, if at all, the previous class activity had affected them. It was dependably cathartic. It was *so* successful, I even got hate mail from absolutist parents!

ILLUSTRATION 'B':

My friends and I were eight. It was a sleepover birthday party for Mark, my best friend. There were five of us boys in all. At nine o'clock, we were sent to Mark's room fortified with cake, chips, hot dogs on sticks and drinks – the idea being that unless we were bleeding, we were there for the night.

We made ready for bed, though we had no intention of going to sleep. I was fascinated and pointed it out. Mark wore PJs, Billy wore PJ's over his underwear, Jack just wore his underpants and Pete wore underpants and undershirt. I preferred sleeping in my skin. We talked about it and decided we'd each try it like each of the others for fifteen-minute periods as we went about playing board games, cards and listening to the radio.

In the end, we each were convinced *our* original way was right for us, but the others really weren't wrong. (Even at that age, I understood in my home there were very few absolute rights (love) and wrongs (killing). We agreed we could still be friends – 'children will lead the way?' We finished the cake, the chips, the hotdogs, and the Coke, then took turns throwing up as night turned into morning.)

DISCUSSION:

Judging others according to predetermined standards precludes the objective examination of things like intent and allows no relevance of one's past experiences, traditions, reasons, needs, and so on. It opens the portal to labeling a person as bad or good based only on the behavior and no supplemental information – because there can be no relevant supplemental data for the absolutist. If you do "A" you are bad or guilty and no additional information can change that.

"He read Mein Kompf, therefore his is a Nazi."

"He believes in universal healthcare; therefore, he is a Socialist."

"She dated Danny, so she has to be a slut."

"Tommy slept in his skin, so he is bad."

I think it was Thumper's mother who told him if he couldn't say something nice about somebody, to not say anything at all. My mother went a step further indicating that we must reserve making judgments about people until we have all the relevant information. Of course, how an absolutist defines *relevant information* will be different from the more open among us.

When my son was in his early teens, he went through a period when he wanted to spend time with boys who had 'bad' reputations. I told him that he could do that with the one stipulation that he would only do it at our house. He gave us his word – all that was necessary. Partly, that was for his safety, and partly for his mother's and my peace of mind. We encouraged them to eat with us and join in our family conversations, even stay the night.

Our son soon understood the considerable contrast between us and them – our beliefs, our ways, our values, with theirs. He saw where theirs got them and where ours got us without us having to preach a single sermon. None of those friendships (my wife called them 'whatifships') lasted long and after a few months he had discovered whatever he had originally set out to investigate. His former friends were happy to have him return to the fold.

We can't preach openness unless we consistently demonstrate it, can we?

IMPLICATION:

Many of the problems between parents and teens form around matters of absolutes – right and wrong, good and bad, appropriate and inappropriate. Absolutist *rules* must be added to that mix.

Teen: "I don't see why I can't ever stay out past ten on Friday nights." (The absolute rule.)

Father: "What do you want to do that requires you be out after ten?"

Teen: "Be with my friends."

Father: "With their parent's permission – a call to your mother or me – they are welcome to be here in the house with you until midnight on Friday nights. (My grandfather had pointed out to me that for teenage boys, nothing good ever transpired after midnight.) We will find ways to make sure you have your privacy

– you can rearrange the basement to fit your needs. We can get in pop and snacks if they will chip in and help with those expenses. Air, water, keester stations, and space will be free."

It worked in our home. After a few months it dribbled to an occasional get together.

In the world view, religion – absolutist religion – poses the largest threat to man's survival.   Read most any cultural anthropologist and he or she asserts and confirms that. When religion comes down to *our* beliefs are right, and *all others* are wrong, it seems to easily move to, 'since ours is right and yours is wrong, people adhering to your beliefs must convert or be killed.' Not much room for 'humanity-saving' moves in that sort of atmosphere, is there?

The open-minded approach is to agree each has his right to his beliefs so long as they don't hurt anyone. The closed-minded approach disallows opposing views, so there is no room for peace and the anthropologists will have been proved right. A similarly disruptive thing happens within politics when views of the parties are absolute and disparate. Examine the so called Banana Republics – even certain, frightening, movements in the US.

CONCLUSION:

There can be no negotiation between absolutists. The end result depends on the fervor the adherents attach to each belief system. 1) They could live side-by-side acknowledging they will never make the time and effort to learn about each other. 2) One can dominate the other, limiting or eliminating the practices of the other. 3) More or less violent confrontation may occur destroying one or the other, or most likely, significant portions of both.

At the less extreme level, we all have met the know-it-all – irksome but typically not a planet-threatening type. The two are cut from the same cloth, however.

Folks who insist on holding absolutist views simplify their lives; 'since I am right, I have no need to learn about any other way' – they embrace intentional ignorance.

We grow by learning new things. That not only *requires* positive openness, but it *fosters* positive openness. Continued personal growth provides the most reasonable path toward saving humanity. Cutting humanity off from personal growth surely will lead to its destruction.

* * * * *

VALUE PAIR EIGHTEEN:
Finding purpose and happiness through integrity
rather than
seeking it through stuff, status, or power

ILLUSTRATION:

Teddy was fourteen, small in stature, blue eyes, dirty blond unkempt hair that hung down to his collar. He had one of those wonderful smiles that made you know he was either a saint or a conman. Everybody in high school knew Teddy – they all offered him smiles, high fives, words as they passed in the hall. He once described himself to me like this: "I'm everybody's friend but I don't have any friends. The kids I'd like to hang with don't take me seriously and the kids who let me in aren't the kind I'm comfortable with. A guy's gotta have somebody, though, you know?"

It was really a question – "I'm drowning, here. What can I do?"

Like many teens I counseled, he thought he didn't dare be seen with me – after all, I worked with the kooks – a real status killer among their peers. Still, he wanted a relationship. I would be walking in the hall or on a sidewalk downtown on Saturday and would hear a voice behind me. It always began in the same way – a whisper; "Teddy here. Don't look around."

He would then ask a question or deliver some piece of news he believed I needed to know: "Billy's back to drinking again," "Adam and Jake are going to have it out under the bridge at ten, tonight – there may be knives," and so on. He'd be gone as quickly as he arrived. In my journal, I called him *T. the Shadow Boy.*

Sometimes it would be good news; "Jerry's stopped threatening Neal about hanging with Jane. He's sweet on the new girl from Rockford."

I had lots of connections within the culture of wayward teen

97

males and with his information I was usually able to derail the most serious of the situations.

The assistant principal had dubbed the group of marginal boys, *The Rouges*. They probably didn't know what it meant but were willing to accept the status they believed it bestowed upon them. With the name, came more and more discomfort for Teddy – *The Rogues* made it sound like a gang. He wasn't into being a gang member regardless of the status it automatically assigned among some – he just wanted to hang with somebody.

One weekend, I was out of town at a meeting. I got back late Sunday night. There was a stone on my front step – a signal from Teddy that he was waiting for me out of sight around back. I went to meet him. He was huddled next to the cement slab steps, back against the foundation. It was dark, but it took no light to determine he was sobbing. I knelt beside him and gently sat him up into the light. His bloody T-shirt was torn to shreds. His face was bruised and bloody. One eye was swollen shut. He was holding his stomach. There were deep abrasions across his throat. The lad had nearly had the life beaten out of him.

I helped him inside and cleaned him up so I could determine the true extent of the damage. His story was straightforward: The Rogues were drunk. They had a gun. They were determined to go to the assistant principal's house and shoot him. Understanding all that, the part that resided deep inside that boy – the part that made decisions between right and wrong – his way or not his way – began screaming at him. The choices were immediately clear: 1) run away from them, stay out of it, remain safe, loose them as pals, and have the VP end up dead when he opened his front door, *or* 2) see that somebody intervened. My back wasn't available for him to talk to.

He understood nobody took him seriously – students, teachers, police, parents. He found the boys as they were putting the final touches on their necessary state of inebriation. Nobody knows what words he used to try and dissuade them other than it included something about having already called the cops – he hadn't, but it was something he figured would put a stop to the plan. Those were not the words the Rouges wanted to hear – the beating ensued.

I called the man to make sure he was well and alert him to the danger. I contacted Teddy's mother and a doctor friend who arranged for an ambulance, which delivered him to the hospital for a seven day stay. Members of the Rogues – not the brightest bulbs in the room – bragged to a few girls they wanted to impress, and the authorities commandeered their lives for the next eighteen months.

That night, Teddy had to choose between the only 'friends' he had in the world and doing the thing he believed was right. He figured he had no good solution to the problem so, even understanding the possible outcome for himself, he did the only thing he knew to do – attack it head on. His plan had been to head from the gathering to the assistant principal's home and alert him.

The point of the story was summed up in the boy's first words to me after he returned to his room from surgery: "I'd do it, again, you know? I would!"

Although he couldn't tell you what the word *integrity* meant, he had just become its living definition – he stood by his positive beliefs, regardless. He is one of my heroes!

DISCUSSION:

I once thought of integrity as meaning 'having a set of values and never wavering from exhibiting them or living up to them.' I have modified that to, 'having a set of *positive* values . . .' Otherwise, the worst of the mobsters could have a high degree of integrity – that's not what I'm after. It is a defining positive trait – the thing other people point to as the best positive descriptor of somebody.

In his way, Teddy was determined to hold the world together one incident at a time. He had a strong sense of what was right because in his home most everything was wrong. He was one of the few who was perceptive enough to understand he should *not* model what was going on around him. As the fifth of five troubled children, he had the 'advantage' of seeing the devastating long-term effects of carrying on the 'family traditions'. Did I mention, he is one of my heroes?

IMPLEMENTATION:

I always resisted telling a youngster how he should solve a problem or resolve a conflict unless it involved stopping blood flow. I found a more effective, long-lasting, approach was to ask, "What is going to make things best for everybody involved in the long run?" It was not an 'ask and respond' question – it demanded analytic and compassionate thinking over a period of time.

Implementation? Back to the old standby – model integrity in every act your child or student sees. Like in telling a lie to a child, there is often no 'fixing' an ill-conceived response *tomorrow*. Consistency, consistency, consistency.

CONCLUSION:

Maintaining a flourishing mankind well into the future, demands the belief in and the regular demonstration of consistent, socially positive values and protective measures – integrity based in positive social values. Anything less will allow – or, direct, even – the demise and death of mankind. There are pockets of humanity that survive and thrive because of the Positive Social Values on which their society or sub-society is based. There are also an abundance of 'anti-survival' processes underway. Have you noticed how seldom it is that those positive pockets of humanity invade and do ill to the harmful pockets? [My novel, *Envisaging an Ideal Society*, speaks to the interplay, and suggests a strategy for survival in the apparent face of inevitable doom.]

* * * * *

VALUE PAIR NINETEEN:
Youngsters having adult confidants,
rather than
only having peer confidants

ILLUSTRATION:

Back in my psychologist days, I spent several hours a week at the county juvenile detention center – I still shudder that any institution should require such a name in a civilized country such as ours. I was often asked to meet with a new teenage resident and make program recommendations. There was one part of my report I could have always written before I even met them – I didn't, but I could have – the boy was close to *no* adult male with a positive outlook on living, and he spent ninety-five plus percent of his free, waking hours hanging with other troubled boys his age – give or take 12 months – who had nothing constructive to do with their lives. When asked who he confided in or consulted with for advice, it would always be a peer – virtually never anything close to an upstanding adult. When asked whose advice he trusted the most, peers always won the day – the tougher the more likely. When asked who he distrusted the most, adults in suits and ties came in first. My first recommendation was also relatively automatic in those reports – 'Somehow, get an acceptable, responsible man into his life'.

We would do an exercise together: I'd pose a personal problem a boy his age might face and ask him what he thought an age-mate would advise. Then, I'd have him verbalize the trail that advice would require him to follow – where would he end up? If it were a bad place, I'd have him ask me for my advice and I'd provide it. He'd again follow the trail. The possible outcomes that he discovered were always better if not entirely trusted. He would demonstrate that he had no idea how to formulate a problem so it could be stated with precision. We'd roleplay back and forth. There would be further discussion. The boys reacted as if I had just sprinkled magic pixie dust on them. Leaning how to formulate problems so they had some chance of being solved! Rehearsing probable consequences before acting. Planning ahead! Personal problems could be resolved in helpful ways. Who'd a thunk?

Once the super-defensive, 'me and my friends can figure stuff out' veil was dropped, it took little doing for the boy to understand which alternative source for advice was probably most reliable and why. (This was a semi-rural Midwestern area in the US.) He could readily see that folks with experience, knowledge, and wisdom, and who remained on the right side of the law would offer the best advice. What person fit that bill – an adult, not another kid. Good progress, huh? Not so. It almost always brought the boys around to the same point – "I don't have any grown-up like that I can go to."

Let me offer a brief, real-life example from forty years ago, so, paraphrased, of course:

Carl was a short-term foster son in my home – fifteen, far brighter than he realized, fairly verbal, virtually unsupervised since that morning he left home for kindergarten. His pals were his whole life. (Not unusual at fifteen.) His pals were always in trouble. (*That*, was unusual.) I can't say I even remember how he came to the attention of the Juvenile Judge. It doesn't matter.

New boys that came to us straight from juvenile court typically tried a runaway the first night in our home. I had a standard approach. In the hall, outside his door on a chair, I left him a note.

If you are running away, I have fixed sandwiches and chips for you to take along – brown bag in the refrigerator. If you take a blanket – it will be chilly this evening – please find a way to return it – blankets are expensive. Hope to see you at breakfast in the morning – I'm thinking pancakes and sausage. Do you prefer butter or honey butter on your toast?

In all those years, only one ever missed breakfast.

Carl was in school during the day but was on 'lockdown' at my home the rest of the time – unless he and I had an outing of some kind – we managed quite a few. We talked as I drove him to school, mornings. We talked when I got home afternoons. We talked in the evenings. At the outset, he was content to take the required stab at the questions I asked and, halfheartedly, engage the topics I offered. He could play the game. Gradually, he had questions to ask me. Shortly, we were having meaningful exchanges – some quite philosophical, in fact.

At the end of the fourteen days he spent with us, the Family Service Social Worker arrived to move him to his permanent foster home across town. At the door, he reached out to shake my hand – something new between us.

"Thanks for talking to me – especially that 'blanket note'. I learned three main things: how dumb my friends are, how smart I am, and that you and I are both okay. I never just talked with a man before like that. Can you believe that? Never! Is there some way we can still do that sometimes?"

We worked it out. (For the sentimental among us, his first child is named Thomas.)

DISCUSSION:

The United States has the highest (by far) number of 'single mother with child' homes in the developed world (W.H.O.). It makes me weep – here in the United States of America. Some 80 percent of juvenile crime is committed by youngsters from single parent homes. Some 70 percent of adult, non-white-collar crimes, are committed by those who came from single parent homes. [Stats vary from time to time and place to place. The trend is the point.]

I am not here to blame single mothers; I am here to state the facts. Boys and girls – boys especially – need a stable man in their lives. Have some kids without that made it? Of course. I have had the pleasure of knowing many remarkable single mothers. Early in my career they taught me a good deal. I'm speaking in typical terms.

Advice will almost always be worse from teen peers than from a thoughtful man. Unfortunately, even a good woman's advice seldom stands up against the advice from a boy's male peers.

A world filled with adults who raised themselves on the advice of poorly informed peers, will be rocky at best, devastating, most likely.

IMPLEMENTATION:

Well led organizations like Scouts, Boy's and Girl's clubs, musical and artistic groups, and organized and after school sports have saved more young lives from distress and social failure than can be imagined. *Quality* foster care can certainly turn kid's lives around. Likewise, for Big Brother and Sister programs – mentoring programs in general.

The problems built into volunteer mentoring programs, stem from the high turnover of adult companions and leadership. Inconsistency and abandonment from those adults the kids have envisioned as promising to be there for them is devastating. Short termers, like interns from college sociology or adolescent psychology classes, offer hope and then withdraw it at the end of the semester or after they have put in their 24 hours. The volunteers' good intentions often leave sadness and distrust in their wake.

When a family adopts a dog, they are told it must be a forever commitment. No such cautions are given when 'well intentioned' adults rush in to interact positively with *mis*advantaged children. I don't have the answer. I have a lot of cautions. I suppose, to be honest with the child at the outset about both the nature and the likely length of the association, is essential. And for the volunteer, never over-commit. That signals to most 'system' children that no adult should ever be counted on. That sets the bar pretty low for himself as he grows to manhood.

CONCLUSION:

The data shows that children need reliable, long-term adults in their lives; adults that can be trusted to be there for the long-haul. Be innovative. Perhaps, have a small *group* of adults take on the same child so he can feel supported by and comfortable with any or all of them – arrange things so at most any time at least one of them can be available during periods of need. Add a boy or girl to a summer ball team or cycling team; welcome them into a little theater group or instrumental group, or an art class, or . . .

Kids without reliable adults in their lives too often become adults with no rudder – no purpose, no 'mirror', no model or source of positive social values to fall back on in moments of crisis.

That sort of preparation for life seldom builds a society that will survive in a positive manner.

* * * * *

VALUE PAIR TWENTY:
Reconciliation
rather than
Revenge

ILLUSTRATION:

Suggested by an actual situation – 1990 – medium sized city.

Monty Worth, eighteen, along with several generations of his family, lived along 149th street *one* block north of Beaumont Avenue – not the slums but not much better.

Kurt Doran, eighteen, along with several generations of his family, lived along 149th street, *two* blocks north of Beaumont Avenue – a somewhat better neighborhood than the one a block south.

Monty had a seventeen-year-old brother – *Chris* – he was the only reservoir of common sense within either family.

Kurt had a younger brother – *Willy* – who worshiped Kurt.

During a robbery of the *Worth Family's Deli*, Kurt shot and killed the father of Monty and Chris. Enraged, Monty went hunting for Kurt and shoved a shiv into his upper left back, killing him.

That wouldn't do. Things couldn't be left at that. Willy and his cousin set up an ambush for Monty and his uncle. They mowed them down with automatic weapons. Outraged, five of Monty's relatives searched for any Doran they could find and a week later, seven of them occupied slabs at the county morgue.

Chris Worth – the most sensible of the lot – went to the police and explained what was going on – a revenge war that would never end unless a stop was put to it there and then. He explained his plan. Under police protection, Chris sat down with all the young Dorans and Worths – one at a time – trying to help them see the folly in the escalation of the feud. No matter how much more killing there might be, it could never solve the problem – both families would live in fear and growing sorrow forever. Was that what the families wanted for their children? That provided the fragile breakthrough – the kids.

105

After a month of conversations, the families agreed to stop the violence unless seriously provoked. There would be no handshakes – no forgiving and forgetting. Chris required that there would be no contact between the families because each came with hair trigger tempers as original equipment. One blink, one sneer, one unacceptable move might well start it all over again. Each family grieved over its losses and avoided each other's territory. The hate had not dissipated – the killing had.

Continuing to have operated according to the *Revenge Motive* would have resulted in running blood baths across two square city blocks, never leading to a solution – 'one of us will get two of you and then two of you will get four of us and on and on forever'. Revenge, unbridled, always escalates; it never solves or even reduces a conflict.

Phrases such as, "Don't get mad, get even," are absolutely terrible advice. They legitimize revenge and boil the pot, if, usually at a less intense level. Revenge never solved a problem. It should not occupy a line on the menu of possible responses. That requires alternatives – alternatives many neighborhoods do not possess. It leaves a terrifying open question, doesn't it?

[Note: My novel, *12 Doors to Pass*, develops the contention that Revenge always makes things worse for all concerned. My, did it make things worse in *that* instance.]

DISCUSSION:

To an outsider who is watching the Revenge Motive play out, it is immediately seen to be folly. Those on the inside, filled with anger and passion and grief and irrational commitment, almost never do. 'We must retaliate, whether to take revenge or to maintain our honor – makes no difference.' It is not a process triggered by either common sense or looking forward to the wellbeing of one's group.

IMPLEMENTATION:

The approach Chris used, above, is the one most often found to be helpful. First, it involves one of their own. It ties the solution, the 'new approach', to the future and leaves what was, behind. Not easy. Often not successful especially in situations where separation is not possible or practical.

In families and neighborhoods committed to problem solving and reconciliation, revenge never becomes a consideration. Modeled early and consistently, problems are attacked logically and examined factually from all sides.

It comes down to solution vs punishment. Homes based in punishment are hotbeds for revenge. Homes based in learning-based solutions, are most likely to solve the problems and move ahead, everybody the wiser. Where homes remain impotent, schools and other agencies must step up and offer – model – the methods for peaceful, reasonable, solutions. [Detention and suspension almost never improve things – they are both negative approaches and how does the Deep Mind deal with negatives?]

CONCLUSION:

Unbridled revenge destroys a sizeable portion of the primary folks and inevitably inflicts much collateral damage. We need to reconsider the punishment base of our judicial system – do we just want punishment (society's revenge) or do we want reliable change so what happened won't happen again? (There are probably a 'billion' books on that topic, alone, and still look at where society still finds itself.)

True, some bad guys will just always remain bad guys. Many – most, even – will modify their approach to living when *given* hope, oppertunity, and the tools – one of which, of course, is commitment to a set of Positive Social Values. I say 'given', which is a false characterization, of course. It is 'when a person sees the necessary, personal, *significance – advantage –* of them' that the stable, long term change comes. The long-term differences in their lives are accomplished through love rather than hate, altruism rather than greed, fair treatment and honesty rather than dishonesty and deceit. Having to live in fear, on the street, often cancels all the other positive factors.

A society based even partly on revenge (Unfortunately, the way human society has most always, been) is bound to lead toward its own destruction – period.

* * * * *

VALUE PAIR TWENTY-ONE:
Knowing one is a worthy being
rather than
having to keep trying to prove one is a worthy being.

ILLUSTRATION:

My child clinical psychology practice was divided evenly among my work in the schools, my work with patients whose parents could comfortably pay for my services, and those who could not pay. This is a story of Mark who fell into the latter category. He had come to my attention through both the school and the local juvenile officer. The words used here, of course, represent the gist of my recollections. The essence is accurate.

I needed written permission from parents to provide my services to those I 'picked up' from the street. I remember quite vividly *that* part of the encounter with Mark's father.

"I need your signed permission in order to spend time with your son."

I offered the form and a pen.

"I'll sign anything. If you have a paper that lets me give him to you, I'll sign that, too."

Mark was with us in the room. He gave no particular response to his father's remark. I turned to the boy – fourteen, short, and thin as a rail.

"I haven't had breakfast yet. How about coming along and we can see if *Melvin's Truck Stop* out on the highway has anything we might like?"

It was well away from where he'd be seen with me by anybody who mattered to him. The drive gave us fifteen minutes to ease into a relationship. I understood he still might take off across a cornfield to escape. That made those fifteen minutes of initial bonding crucial.

He didn't offer two dozen words that morning, but had no difficulty putting away a breakfast of steak, eggs, hash browns,

109

and toast.

He had ordered black coffee but had barely sipped at it – a macho ploy, I suspected.

"After coffee, I often like a glass of milk. How about you, Mark?"

He nodded, head still low, sneaking peeks at my face out of the top of his eyes. I could only imagine the confusion and reluctance brewing inside his head – fear, even.

"I'm late for school," he offered at last.

"I've arranged it, so you're excused this morning. I figured that would give us time to begin getting to know each other."

"You can do that?"

"I can. I did."

He was clearly impressed and sat up a bit straighter.

"You like to spend time at the river?"

About the only personal thing I knew about him was that he enjoyed fishing.

I got a nod.

When we arrived, I asked him to pick a spot where we could sit, suggesting he knew the place far better than I did. (Recognizing the other as the expert, typically moves a relationship in the desired direction.) He moved us twice – a test of some sort. I think I passed having indicated no objection and offering mild praise for each of his choices.

Eventually, he asked the crucial question.

"What are you doing?"

"You understand it's no secret you've been in a lot of trouble lately. Lots of people who care about you are concerned."

"Nobody cares about me."

He *could* say things with conviction.

I ignored it and continued.

"One of my interests is to help guys your age get things sorted out so they can leave that kind of stuff behind and get on with a happy life."

"I'm happy."

"No, you aren't."

It was purposefully more forceful than anything I had said up to that moment.

Miffed, he stood and walked away, perhaps thirty yards. I didn't follow or even call after him – in fact, I turned slightly so I was facing away from him. He walked a circuitous path back to where I was and sat down, legs crossed beneath him. We had our first substantive talk – lots of testing – excuses, big lies, small lies, scape-goating, limit testing. There were several references to how he hated me nosing into his life and that he'd never talk with me again.

I dropped him off at school in time for lunch.

During much of the next thirteen months, he continued to get into minor trouble – much of it clearly to get noticed (court appearances kept his father involved in his life) – he'd brag about it, assuming that provided status among his associates. Sometimes he tried to make it my fault. I wouldn't buy into his line but never argued against his contention. We talked often. He did what he could to manipulate and use me. In most instances, I managed it for his benefit – not always what he wanted or expected. We had lots of meals together – a few picnics at the river. In the winter we went sledding and ice skating. I showed him how to fish through the ice – a skill I had acquired when I lived in New York. We burned one end of a fence post to a glowing point then set it vertically atop the ice and let it melt an eight-inch hole through to the water. He really got into that! He seldom indicated that he enjoyed our time together. He did!

Testing, testing, testing – ringing my doorbell for a talk at two a.m. I set things up so he could demonstrate his skills to me – the ice fishing, swimming, math. He worked on some do-it-yourself projects I provided – beading a belt, making a working clock with a pendulum, moccasins, even a few more serious art activities. At first, he insisted he didn't want to work on my dumb projects. Eventually that changed to, "I'll probably need some help with this one", and later to requesting stops at the craft shop to see what new things they had.

Over time, his vocabulary, grammar, and speech pattern began mimicking mine. His teachers noticed and at my suggestion they gently let him know – just recognition of the improvement – not enough to scare him off. Most notably, they reported his temperament had mellowed. During the final six or so months of our relationship, he had stopped swearing for effect at school as well as when he was with me. He had been the detention king – that stopped entirely a few months into our relationship – detention cut into our afterschool time together. On occasion, he even asked for advice – as much to test it as to follow it.

A few months into his sophomore year he and his father moved halfway across the country. He didn't tell me of the plan until the day he left.

Years passed. No letters. No communication. I moved on – sadly, there were always others waiting in line. It wasn't that I didn't wonder about him often.

Seven years later, a small, flat, package arrived in the mail. I opened it. At first, I didn't understand. It was a plaque and read: *This plaque is presented by the Young Christian Businessmen's Association of the Greater Dallas/Ft. Worth area, recognizing Mark Smith as our Man of the Year, for his tireless work with the disadvantaged young men in our community.*

There was a handwritten note – brief and to the point: 'This is the most precious thing I've ever had, and I want you to have it. Thanks for helping me believe in myself. Mark'

Often, it doesn't take much; mostly patient, consistent, positive modeling, and allowing the youngster to prove his worth to himself. Believe me. If Mark could make it, that kid down the street can make it, too – with a few opportunities and a nudge here or there and, a l o t of patience.

DISCUSSION:

When your father suggests he'd like to give you to the first man who shows an interest in you, we can believe the kid has had few if any experiences that made him believe in his own worth. Once convinced you're worthless, it becomes your job to keep proving it to yourself and others. 'If that's how dad sees me, I can at least prove to him that he's right.' If he won't pay attention to me, I'll do things that require him to pay attention – at least to acknowledge I'm alive. Mark had become proficient at those things.

Words don't change a youngster who has reached that stage, so 'traditional' talk therapy was no place to start. I used what I called Relationship Therapy. It's essence was illustrated above. For months he was sure I was trying to trick him into something – it bothered him that he couldn't figure out what it was. Once 'bothered' morphed into 'intrigued', the relationship became relatively smooth – cordial, maybe even trusting.

I chose activities that were foreign to him – crafts and art projects – because he had no record of failing at them. There was no little reluctance. As I recall, I completed the first one by myself while he watched – a miniature birchbark canoe on a display base. On the second, while he was watching, I made a few initial errors on purpose and he corrected me, showing me how it should have been done. With that, he was hooked. I chronicled the rest above.

IMPLICATION:

When you *know* you're no good, you don't try be good at anything. Success would attack your self-concept; failure would confirm that the worst about you might really be true. That makes sense in a way. However, when self-worth is merely dependent on a general, positive, picture reflected back at you by somebody you come to believe, then, wonderful, positive changes can begin to happen. And, so it seems to have been. Consider the ultimate result for Mark if the juvenile system had taken its typical route and punished him time and time again for his 'self-unworth-proving misadventures'.

CONCLUSION:

A world populated by folks who believe, 'I know I'm no good so it would be wasted effort to try', provides little hope mankind will be able to work toward an improved human condition. Early in life, Mark really had tried to please his father – many times every day. He was pushed aside and called a nuisance, a looser, trouble, get out from underfoot. Later, he set about proving his father's image of him as an incompetent, bothersome, boy – he would gain his approval one way or the other – if not approval, at least his attention every time the principal called, or the cops brought him home. Have we ever seen a 'human group' that knew they were no good, that led us toward a better existence?

Those of us who choose to try and save humanity, must help children (and adults) prove their self-worth to themselves every day of their lives. Make sure they have things at which they can succeed. We wouldn't put a student who can only read at a third-grade level into a book that required 8th grade skill (would we? Yes, we would if every child in the class has the same reader). Kind words and positive support – *when it is clearly deserved* – helps – but seeing it and feeling it and being able to verbalize it is the true test for all of us.

What a world we could produce if we all went to sleep at night knowing we were worthy, capable, human beings, very likely to succeed at whatever we tried that next day. Would we not be ready to crawl out and take on the world with renewed hope and vigor every single morning?

* * * * *

VALUE PAIR TWENTY-TWO:
A user of precise language
rather than
imprecise Language

ILLUSTRATION:

[The first session with an eleven-year-old boy referred by his new foster mother who was concerned about his constant swearing, in my characterization, his *lazy language*. There are several forms of lazy language.]

ME: Willy. Why did Mrs. Branson bring you to talk with me, today?

W: She's got some kind a damn problem with how I talk.

ME: Some kind? Surely, she was more specific than that.

W: She don't like my cussing.

ME: How do *you* feel about your cussing?"

W: What do you mean?

ME: How does it make you feel when you cuss?"

W: [He shrugged] No different than saying other words, I guess. What you going to do if I cuss here?

ME: Most likely, I'll be honest with you and say I don't understand what you *really* mean. And by the way, you already cussed.

He looked down into his lap and then up at me.

W: I don't get it.

ME: Listen to these two sentences:

>I hate the damn music class.

>I don't like music class because I was never taught how to read music.

If I only heard you say the first one, I would have no way of knowing what you *really* mean.

W: Maybe you're wrong. Maybe it's because the teacher's mean to me.

ME: See there, how you just cleared it up by using 'meaningful words'. Now that I know that, I might be able to help you have a better time in music class. I would have never known that from the sentence that substitutes the lazy word – all cuss words are lazy words – because they don't say what's really on your mind. They always reveal that you didn't take time to think through what was *really* on your mind – lazy, see? Let's say I hear three boys call Mr. Mack a GD teacher. Do you think each boy means the same thing by GD?"

W: Maybe not.

ME: Will you explain that to me? You're very good with examples."

He sat up a bit straighter, beginning to buy into my process.

W: Say the first boy means the teacher uses big words he don't understand. Maybe the second boy don't like him because he makes the boy stay after school to get his homework done. Maybe the last boy thinks the teacher hates him. (I suppose we don't have to look far to see where those 'possibilities' came from.)

ME: Good examples, Willy. That presents a big problem, doesn't it."

W: What do you mean?

ME: When each of the boys means something different when he uses the same words, the teacher has no idea what they mean when they swear about him, does he?

W: He should. Most teacher suck.

ME: Once again, I have no idea what you mean when you say they suck – they are mean, they talk too fast, they use words you don't understand, they won't help you, they are boring, they hate you, they are unfair to you? See where I'm going with this?

W: Yeah.

ME: Tell me what we have learned about swearing in the past sixty seconds.

I smiled to myself as he looked at his watch as if to check.

W: [He assumed an impish grin.] That it *sucks*?

ME: [I met his grin and raised him a chuckle.]
I can tell I'm going to enjoy your blinkin' sense of humor, young man.

W: What do you mean – blinkin'? Oh. You're sneaky.

ME: In fact, you will soon learn I am plooty blinkin' sneaky.

W: Okay. Okay. What you're saying is that a swear word covers up what I really mean.

ME: Because?

W: Let's see, because the swear word can mean a million

different things. It's like solving for X in an equation – you can't know what it means until you take the time to work the problem.

ME: That's an excellent example! I'll bet you that sometimes when you say something like, 'I hate the plooty blinkin' assignment', you're using those words because you aren't quite sure what you don't like about the assignment – you haven't taken enough time to figure out what bothers you about it. In that case, neither the teacher *nor* you knows what the deal is. I'm sure you've had times like that, right?

W: I guess. I thought Mrs. Branson was just mad at me because I said bad words in front of Sammy – her three-year-old. I think you're missing something, though, Doc."

I love moments like that.

ME: "Please tell me what that is."

W: Sometimes when I swear the worst, it's like I'm building up a wall to keep somebody away from me – keep them from bothering me or coming after me or maybe questioning something I did or said. The words don't matter none.

ME: Like a wall of frightening power – your private force field to keep the other person at a safe distance?

W: Right! You know stuff, don't you?

He seemed truly mystified that I understood.

Mrs. Branson said you were good.

He moved to the front of his chair, hands folded across his knees.

You know what me and you outta do?

ME: What? I'm eager to hear."

I moved forward to meet him.

W: We outta write a book about this stuff so other kids could learn about it. I got a great title: *Giving Up Lazy Language for Fun and Profit*. That's great, right?"

ME: Blippity great, I'd say.

W: [He laughed himself onto the floor – the very best sort of laughter for an eleven-year-old boy.]

ME: I think it's time you and I negotiated a deal.

W: What sort of a deal?"

He righted himself – still halfway forward on the chair – indicating his heightened level of interest.

ME: One blippity kerplunket deal.

W: Definitions please.

ME: 'Really cool'

W: I don't never make deals 'til I see all the cards.

ME: Here they are, then. You will keep a list of all the times you use a swear word this week and translate it into what you believe you meant. You will keep a second list of the times you caught yourself and substituted a useful word for the lazy word you were thinking of using.

W: Can they be on the front and back of the same page?

WE: Sounds efficient. Something I'd expect of you, even. Sure.

W: So far, I really don't see no margin in that for me. No payoff.

ME: Here it comes. You do a good job on those lists for a full week – seven days – and you and I will write that book you suggested.

W: Really? My name on the front?"

ME: Your name anywhere you want it.

W: And yours of course. Can I start making notes about things I think should go in it before I finish those lists?

ME: I think that would be a blinkity, I mean, a *fine* thing.

A smile and a chuckle.

W: Don't tell Mrs. Branson about it, Okay? I want it to be a surprise the day I hand her the first copy.

ME: I imagine the book will only be a dozen or so pages. You understand that – you okay with that?

W: I do. That don't matter none. I bet there ain't very many guys my age to writ a book – you think?

ME: I'm sure you're right. Remember you have two obligations to live up to during this next week. Two lists. Got that?"

W: Sure. [He became sober, thoughtful.]

ME: What's up?

W: I think this is going to be scary. It's like I'm a cop with all my ammunition taken away from me.

ME: When you phrase things like that, I'm more and more convinced you have the necessary stuff inside you to become a writer if you decide you want to be. A big job of a writer is to keep thinking of better words than the ones he already has down on paper. You are going to be very good at this.

W: I hope you're right about that. I'd really hate to have to blippity grinje your plooty plicked life. I could get to like you, ya know.

[Another long laugh, perhaps just a bit more anxiety driven

than before. In the end, there were fifty copies of ten pages, 14 point text inside a full color cover. I must admit, the subtitle was not my contribution.]

Giving up Lazy Language for Fun and Profit
Lay lazy in the hole; make precision your goal

By Willy Jackson
and Tom Gnagey

Family of Man Press

Publication and Copywrite 2009

ISBN: 0-03-814XXX-1 pbk

[NOTE: Remember that Deep Mind we've discussed, and how it requires simplicity to understand communication. Remember that it uses words quite poorly. Remember how strong emotion helps set directives in the 'easy to find and use section'. When it receives a message about a blippin' Librarian, it will go wild until it finds some resolution. Perhaps *the blimp-like librarian*, or *the blinking librarian*, or the *liberal libertarian* or the *liberal from Iberia* – the confusion can go on forever. Perhaps the angry emotion will be all that can be set – right there alongside the concept 'Librarian'. One thing for sure, lazy language always sends ill-defined, confusing messages to the deep mind. Next time we have coffee, ask me about the case of the priest where *'g - d d - - n Kilimanjaro'* got set in place as 'God demands you kill the man, Jerry'. The result was disastrous. (From a real case. Not mine.)

If you are given to profane language, consider a redo. It doesn't prove you are smart as you embark on a thoughtless, willy nilly shuffling of the all-important directives in your deep mind. It proves you'd rather indulge in lazy speech habits than speak with precision and keep your deep mind properly maintained. For some it will demonstrate you want to remain angry rather than understanding it.

DISCUSSION:
Most of the discussion has been presented, above. I'll just

add one tangential item. As I have spent a lifetime studying those who choose to swear, one thing is often clear. It is many people's attempt at saying, "See, I swear. Therefore, I'm just as common as you are. That proves I don't want my position, or my title, or my name to intimidate you." It's like that John Lennon interview in which he spends the time sitting cross-legged on a pillow while picking at his toenails. 'I'm just a common guy.' About all profanity really conveys is that one failed to take seriously his or her mother's admonition not to swear and that there is an admitted ingenuine facet about the person right from the git go.

IMPLICATION:

Compared with users of imprecise language, users of precise language communicate far more effectively with others as well as with the part of their mind that determines most of the truly important things that will happen during their life. It seems important and only smart to communicate ones needs, questions and emotional responses as precisely as possible to one's mind. A confused Deep Mind is dangerous to one's well-being.

(After you, like I, have spent sixty years studying the process, and correcting the damage it does, you may argue with me. Remember, facts, not opinion – especially *defensive* opinion – the most dangerous kind of all, *and* unless you are one whizz of a statistician, don't mention those atrocious, inadequately designed studies that purport to prove people who swear are more intelligent than the rest of us – *A-1 Tommyrot* – smile.)

CONCLUSION:

Make certain you know the precise meaning of the words you choose to use – swear words or others. To the degree possible, use words you feel certain the other person will understand. The most 'perfect' word is not 'precise' if the other person doesn't know what it means. My grandmother urged me to use quarter words rather than nickel words. My grandfather took me aside and said although it was fine and useful to have a stash of quarter words, they were worthless when trying to communicate with folks who only understood nickel words.

In therapy sessions, I would not use the same set of words with a kid off the street as I did with a college professor. The same today on the bus. A world in which precise language is spoken thoughtfully, allows accurate communication to flourish. Imprecise language messes up *everything*. When Jill really means *communism* when she uses the word *socialism* with Mary who thinks *communism* means *fascism*, you got trouble there in River City.

When I was working with pairs or groups of people who were so deep into disagreements that they could no longer communicate, I used a time-proven method. Before a person could respond, he had to restate the previous person's idea – and keep trying until that person agreed it was accurate. So much of miscommunication is due to poor listening skills and not taking time to understand what somebody else means by the words he uses. Always clarify what the other person means by important words – conservative, liberal, generous, unfair, hate, love, socialism, democracy, capitalism, loyalty, patriotic, good, bad, and so on. ALWAYS CLARIFY before proceeding. [*proceeding: moving ahead along a path already established or agreed to*.]

A world trying to communicate with imprecise language has little chance of communicating accurately. Humans depend almost entirely on words for expressing themselves. So, if most of what they do during chats is not a precise representation of what's in their mind, good things can't happen; bad things probably will. I'm not betting a world survives when folks have no good idea what each other mean.

* * * * *

VALUE PAIR TWENTY-THREE:
Cherishing individual freedom
of belief and behavior
rather than
Assuming others must believe
and act like you.

ILLUSTRATION:

By this point in this book, it will come as no shock to the reader that when I was nine, I was asked to leave summer Church Camp and not come back. My parents were informed that I asked the wrong questions, and it bothered the other children. I'm sure it was really Pastor Pauly and Sister Irene who were bothered. The veins in their temples worked their throbbing ways toward the bursting point every morning when my eager, smiling face showed up on the first row ready for class.

"Pastor, please show me in the Bible where it says I must bow my head, fold my hands, and close my eyes while you are praying and then say Amen when you stop."

"I can't."

"Are you saying God won't hear my prayer if I'm standing on my head and whistling – only when I'm kneeling?"

I was objecting to the man's parochial approach – he made it seem that if we kids didn't do everything the way *he* had decided *we* should do it, *we* were in the wrong. (The other kids, by the way, without exception, enjoyed my head-standing approach to religious supplication.) I will just say Pastor should have felt fortunate I was only taking on matters of form and ritual and not the basic beliefs he was presenting to us. By the time he got to that each morning I was probably distracted and experimenting to see how far I could stick my finger down my throat before I threw up. There were so many truly important things to discover.

My parents were devout, religious conservatives. I had

worried that when I would tell them at the end of my freshman year in college, that I had joined the Unitarian Church, they would be hurt. It has been said often: Just when you think you have your parents figured out . . .

I gave them the short speech I had prepared. Grampa always said string out good news but keep bad news short and to the point. Dad responded.

"You are a good person, Tom. That comes from inside you and has very little to do with church membership. A boy's beliefs *should* grow as he carefully acquires new knowledge. So long as yours don't have the intention of hurting anybody and make good sense to you, you have our blessing."

There was a long embrace.

Those were the last words ever spoken over the topic. I must say, I wondered how Pastor and Dad could cherish the same set of basic beliefs and yet be so different as people – Pastor so closed and defensive and Dad so open and genuinely accepting.

Looking back with some care and determination, I realized he had always encouraged me to come to my own decisions about most aspects of life. It wasn't that he wasn't there to help when I asked. I could count on one hand the beliefs he *insisted* I accept – charity for those in need, respect for all flavors of people, love for and stewardship of the planet on which I lived, the right of everybody to hold their own beliefs (providing they hurt no one), and the eager investigation of things new or different.

Our family talked often about beliefs and our hopes and desires for ourselves and others. It was always without judgment. None of that ever seemed *religious* to me. If brother Larry believed in ghosts and brother Bill did not, it was okay. If I put off my decision on that matter until I had grown up, it was okay. As a child, I had been one of God's biggest cheerleaders. My prayer sessions at night out bedazzled a current-day Super Bowl halftime show. By the time I was seventeen, I had lots of questions about the veracity of the God-concept, and I knew that was okay – people were supposed to question and grow. Goodness, it didn't require a belief in a Super-Being to understand that being a good person was the best way to live my life.

When I told grampa about my growing doubts, he said something like this: If the brain God gave you, leads you to question things about Him, that has to be okay, otherwise he wouldn't have given your brain that option."

There were numerous logical inconsistencies in his statement, but it was basically reassuring.

During the summer before my senior year in high school, I set out to make a friend of a boy in my class who I could not figure out – in both beliefs and behavior we seemed to be irreconcilably at odds. I understood my mother was not in favor of it and I'm sure I regularly gave her fear-driven palpations during that year. He had a *bad boy* reputation – yet nobody really warned against him. Let's call him T.J.

One afternoon after summer band practice, I made it a point to pass the time of day with him, while we cleaned up our instruments and put them away. He bought me my first cup of coffee – I tried not to let on. It was, without a doubt, the foulest tasting concoction I had ever held in my mouth. My eyes may have watered! It would not go down and I had no place to put it. I excused myself to the restroom. I'm sure he knew. He didn't say anything. No putdown. No judgement.

He was clearly surprised when I had no problem talking about sex. It had been a test I'm sure he figured goody-goody Tommy would fail. That may have been the clincher from his perspective. It soon became obvious how poor his family was – a mother and younger sister. They always had cigarette money but often not enough to buy milk or bread – like I indicated – humongously different sorts of boys. He was into skin-to-skin, amorous activities with girls; I wasn't. He swore, I didn't. He and his friends drank Saturday nights out under the water tower up on the hill south of town. I would eventually go along but never smoke or drink. He never mentioned it although it was understood. He was far more intelligent than he or anybody realized. The conversations were wonderfully stimulating – he and I talked – the others smoked, drank and threw up. Did I mention we were different?

Despite all of it, he was a person of positive principles: he never stole things; he never vandalized; he was not into taking advantage of others. He was the first to offer help. The more I knew about him the harder it was for me to understand why everybody thought he was a bad boy – a smoker at ten, perhaps?

After I had spent time with him, I, of course, smelled of tobacco smoke. I once overheard my parents discussing that. Mother asked Dad if he thought I was smoking. He said, "Of course he isn't smoking. Tommy wouldn't do that." His 'off camera' response infused my character with strength I still feel today. Knowledge that your hero has complete confidence in you tends to do that.

Mother did convince our Pastor to get me to help him with a church project so he could have a talk with me. In the end, he and I were of the same mind – if I needed to understand my new acquaintance, I needed to get to know him. Remember who I was and go for it. Poor mom! When she was upset, she made me shirts. Win/win, you think? Six before the end of September!

My new friend was honest and likeable though not a leader beyond his small circle of buddies. I was a leader – want me to be or not, I'd find a way to be the leader. I liked being in charge – benevolently, so. Perhaps, that's why to this day I enjoy writing novels having full charge over my characters.

By September, he and I were joined at the hips. We were elected president and vice-president of the senior class. It seemed fitting to every smiling class member that *he* would be president of the *vice.* That year, we learned a good deal about responsibility to ourselves and to others. We both deemed those twelve months together helpful and enjoyable – life changing.

I liked the important parts of him and he, mine – the parts that were left there unadorned once we swept aside the quality of our clothes, the size of our allowances, the standing of our families in the community, and the opportunities that lay ahead. We were most certainly not clones in our beliefs, but we allowed each other what made sense to the other and understood we were growing because of the interplay between us. We loved to laugh and bonded over our sense of justice and fairness and fought against prejudice, outdated tradition, and exclusion. We dreamed great dreams together knowing they would never come to fruition. It was wonderful practice for adulthood. By the time we graduated, we were the best friends either had ever had – neither of us had abandoned our 'old' friends, but clearly, *we* were the *Dynamic Duo of BHS*.

Little known to anyone, he saved my life that summer following graduation and helped me climb out of a deep, dark, pit of depression, back into a functioning eighteen-year-old. I had been the biggest fish in my small pond, and the prospect of having to leave that comfort and security, and go swim in the ocean, which was the world that awaited me, presented unexpected and unexamined terror. After that late-summer experience, we saw each other no more than a half dozen times. Summer ended. Separate goals. Separate opportunities. Separate paths, and separate lives.

He died way too young. I still think about him most every day and have often wondered how my life would be different if I hadn't mustered the courage that afternoon to begin chatting with him in a serious way while I cleaned the spit valve on my trombone and he sucked a new reed to life for his saxophone. My, what I would have missed if I had just stuck with 'my kind'.

[Two of my novels are loosely based on that relationship: 1) *David: a teen boy's search for meaning,* and, 2) *T.J.: a teen boy in search of himself* – they should be read in order since the story continues.]

DISCUSSION:

The United States has long been thought of as a melting pot. Often, that stopped at the idea of ethnicity or country of origin. It must include race, cultures, religious and philosophical beliefs, and family history. Originally, *melting pot* was a synonym for openness. Come one, come all. Improve our country. History tells us that was often more theoretical and fanciful than actual. *People of Difference* have always been excluded and put upon in America. We have never been open, but we tell ourselves we have, to blur and cover our prejudiced past and bolster our 'good guy' self-concepts. Think Italians, Irish, Chinese, Gypsy, Japanese, Germans, Blacks, Mexicans, Middle Easterners – and, of course, Native Americans.

So, the discussion of *openness* as a necessary component of saving humanity, looms large – larger than many of the 22 Positive Social Values we have already discussed. In a world divided into dozens or hundreds of enclaves of intractable, like-minded – like looking – people, we inhabitants of Earth can never achieve the level of mutual understanding that is essential to draw the world together in peace and mutual benefits. Openness encourages understanding, inclusion, and sharing the best we have. Fear, constraint, rejection, and restrictiveness demand separateness.

Ignorance – especially self-imposed ignorance – is perhaps the greatest adversary of inclusiveness. Ignorance is fostered by separation and separation drives ignorance – a vicious, self-fulfilling circle. The all-important, continuing, quest to discover verifiable knowledge, on the other hand, has the potential for alleviating the fear and misgivings that thrive on lore and unsubstantiated rumor and keep folks apart.

IMPLICATION:

Necessary conversations at home explore: 'how are we all alike in our family?' and 'how are we different from each other in our family?' and, 'how do those similarities and differences affect our family?'

"If we were to get an additional family member, what traits might we hope he or she might have that would be useful and interesting and help round out our collective perspective?"

Knowledge of new traits – new possibilities – tend to strengthen a society. They may dilute or modify long-standing guideposts of the society, but, when carefully considered, they tend to improve and expand its wonderful possibilities. The most fearful members of a society will promote a closed society, so ways that have become comfortable for them won't be changed. For a substantial number of us, *comfort*, apparently at the level of our DNA, seems to innately be more acceptable – necessary – than growth and new knowledge.

The bottom-line question may be: Is it best to become stronger by admitting new traits into our society, or wither away and die, just sticking to our comfortable, well established, ways? Other times, the question becomes: the new ideas are inevitable; rather than fight a losing battle and foster growing separateness, how can we thoughtfully include and monitor them in helpful ways?

More and more I am coming to believe that the search for comfort – unabashed, self-centered, comfort – in our lives may become the ultimate downfall of Humanity.

CONCLUSION:

Open societies allow the *consideration* of new ideas that may be helpful or provide guidance toward new opportunities. Closed societies do not and implode on themselves because of it. They keep investing in buggy whips and butter churns. We must encourage thoughtful openness in our children. We must help our children gain accurate evaluation skills that will allow them to separate the grain from the chaff – useful from harmful values and ideas.

A few groups will not think these sorts of progress – changes – are good, because they encourage children to turn their backs on the old ways – often defined as the *good* ways or the *only* good ways. Many, if not most, religious and conservative groups fall into this category and usually reside in absolutist groups that believe they know the TRUTH and that the rest of us don't. That has always been a frightening position to me. Survival, flies in its wake.

* * * * *

VALUE PAIR TWENTY-FOUR:
Democratic approach
rather than
Dictatorial, strong-arm approach

ILLUSTRATION 'A':

With more than twenty years of education under my belt, I have found myself in a wide variety of classrooms. They ranged from strictly dictatorial, teacher directed, to laisses-faire (you have the textbook; come back on December 12th for the final exam.)

I figured I went to the teacher to be directed – at least pointed – to the material he or she, thoughtfully, believed was important. I counted on his or her expertise. Interestingly, that can be achieved anywhere along that philosophic continuum if the student is serious. I preferred the less dictatorial approach in which the important base was presented but further exploration along the lines of my specific interests was recognized and encouraged – master the text and lectures, but do a paper or project that explores your specific interests in some matter related to our field.

Since the reader has had similar experiences, (K to whatever) I won't belabor the topic other than to say the further I went in my education, the more reasonable the 'democratic' approach seemed be. By then, I knew what I needed and had the skills to find it and learn it. Families, like classrooms, must find the most helpful balance between 'democracy' and 'authoritarianism'. It must change, of course, with the maturation of the child – complete authoritarianism as a baby to more liberal democracy as he or she prepares to leave the home.

As the child matures, it becomes essential that he begins taking more and more responsibility for himself – let him make his mistakes while he still has the luxury of a loving, helpful, family to assist and support him. For a successful life in a democracy,

131

education and knowledge are essential – decisions are up to the individual, and *good* decisions are most likely if people know lots of things. In less democratic settings, a broad range of knowledge is seen as a liability, since it is the source of questions and causes discomfort and becomes the agitator for change and the desire for personal liberty. Always be wary when a government regulates, dilutes, or closes down educational opportunities.

ILLUSTRATION 'B'

In 1950, I was in the seventh grade in the small town of Mahomet, Illinois. Twenty busses brought in students from the surrounding rural area. My father was the superintendent of schools. One evening after supper he said he needed my help. My spirit always soared when he asked that. He had something he wanted us to read together. To my surprise it was a comic book – not one I was familiar with, however.

Within its brightly colored pages it purported to present life as it would be in my country if communism should take over. I read it out loud – pointing, frame by frame – as my father sat beside me on the couch. It was a most uncomfortable read, and I wondered what was really going on. Nothing about it was like my parents. We finished.

"So, what did you think of it?" he asked.

I knew I could be honest – that was how we functioned in my family. He would not have asked if he had wanted anything else.

"It scared me. Kids in military uniforms required to tattle on their parents and brothers and sisters if they had reason to be suspicious of their loyalty to the government. It showed parents being taken away from families for thinking the wrong thoughts. It showed large groups of youngsters storming newspapers and buildings of antigovernment movements – ransacking and burning them. It showed families set against families because of their political and religious beliefs. It was really scary."

"How do you respond to the way elections were held?"

"They weren't really elections. Everybody was required to vote for the people who belonged to the communist party. The people really didn't have any say in things."

"What big point did the comic book try to make?"

"Not just *try* – it *showed* how communism is bad and

democracy is good and how we should fight to keep communism out of our lives.”

“Why do you suppose it was produced – the comic book?”

I had to think on that one.

“To frighten kids into wanting to keep our democracy?”

I understood my answer was a question.

“Close enough. Here’s why I had us go through it together. First, I didn’t want you to go through it by yourself for fear it would make you uncomfortable and so I could be here to explain things if you had questions. Second, I have an important question. You see, our government in Washington, D.C. has sent these comic books to all the grade schools in the country with the suggestion every student get one to read. My question to you is, do you think that is a good idea?”

He was using me as an expert – that puffed up my self-worth, I’ll tell you that. I took it on as an important responsibility and presented my reactions one at a time.

“First, it’s way too scary for little kids – below fifth grade, I’d say. Second, it’s hard to believe our government would make something like this. It’s like trying to force us to believe a certain way – just like the communists they are putting down for doing the same thing. Third, I don’t understand what’s behind it. Why hand out something like this?”

I wasn’t finished.

“Okay, so communism is a bad way to govern. And, okay, it gives more examples than most of us kids knew about. But, there’s nothing kids can do about it – we can’t vote and grownups never listen to us anyway when it comes to big things like government and religion. It doesn’t make any suggestions to help us deal with the fear it produces. All it does is scare us forever. I guess that’s my main things. I’m still not sure what you want me to do or why.”

“You have already done it very nicely. You see, it’s my job to decide whether to circulate the comic books in our school or not.”

“So, what did you decide?”

“I agree with everything you have said, but I’m a grown-up – one of those kinds you say never pays attention to kids – so I needed an honest reaction, and I knew you’d give me that.”

We shared a face-to-face smile. I scooted closer to him. He pulled me close. It offered a new, sort of man-to-man bond. I feel it to this day.

"I'm proud of you for the good thinking you have shown this evening. I'm not going to put it out for the students. I will have each teacher prepare a factual discussion and hold a question and response period on the topic. What do you think of something like that?"

I agreed and had suggestions to offer (Tommy ALWAYS had suggestions to offer – after all, it was the duty of the uncrowned King of the World!) I felt a growing sense of importance. It did leave me with a conundrum for future consideration. I knew Dad loved me. Suddenly, I knew he was proud of me. I wondered how they were the same or different – being proud or loving. I needed to know, so I could make it more clear to my son when that time came. It was a discussion for another day.

It had been 'heavy stuff'. I went to my room and retreated into a comic book that was far less discomforting – Captain Marvel in a fight to the death with the Atomic Crimson Banshee.

DISCUSSION:

At eleven, I already understood that human rights and making sure citizens had an important say in government were the basics of a free society. I knew in my home my parents had the final vote on most things, although I recognized the older I became the more say-so I had been allowed in things. That seemed right.

The concept of 'un-freedom' was foreign to me and quite scary. I suddenly understood better the responsibility that full participation in our government would put on my shoulders as an adult – to help decide, by voting, what was best for all Americans. I didn't know 'all Americans', so how could I do that? Ah ha! That's why *everybody* should have a right to speak up, to vote. Later, I learned about the protections minority groups had in a Republic like ours – majority ruled, but minority rights were also protected. I really liked that.

I couldn't imagine assigning my right to freedom to a dictator. I figured the most insecure and uneducated might feel more secure that way – not having the background to handle their own lives. In that way, having a strong person they thought they respected and could trust, probably offered a sense of basic security. It was like when I had been a little kid without the necessary knowledge and skills to survive on my own. Adults who were forced to care for themselves and their families but didn't know how, would probably continue to need a father-like person. It suddenly seemed really important to make sure moms and dads knew how to be moms and dads. Education. It was fodder for more than one sleepless night. (Grampa and I had talked about it.)

IMPLEMENTATION:

Children should be encouraged to practice self-care at levels for which they are competent. This certainly includes decision making and all the important ramifications that implies. Families must see to it, providing ever-expanding opportunities and proper guidance.

I'm sure we agree that it must be the goal of all parents to help their children grow from, "Do it for me," through "help me do it," to "I can do it." Also, that they must gain a realistic sense of their skills relative to their responsibilities. Here, too, there is a more or less genetic difference in folks – some of us are, by nature, dependent and others independent. I am told my first complete sentence was: 'Motty dee eh eye sef!!!' (Tommy will do it myself.) I have no way of verifying that, but what are the chances, do you suppose?)

A common question to children as they move from stage to stage needs to be, "What do you think about ____, and what makes you think that? No evaluation from a grownup is called for. It is the thinking and mental growth that is relevant. Such age-appropriate discussions provide a multitude of essential opportunities for children to expand their sense of right and wrong and understand that opinions can be dangerous if one stops prior to finding fact-based, supportive information. It makes the essential argument for pursuing education – formal and informal – read, read, read.

[A *for-what-it's-worth*, added extra: Each day I make sure I accomplish four things: I do what is required of me; I do something for somebody else, no strings attached; I do something just for me; and I learn something brand new. I believe it has worked pretty well for me. I imagine most of you have similar, daily, goals that you approach regularly.]

CONCLUSION:

Freedom of thought and of appropriate action is essential

to the survival of Humanity – Humanity allowed and encouraged to function and grow toward its finest potential. Those skills find their origins in thoughtful homes that understand about preparing children so they can take good and proper care of themselves and those whose lives they touch. A wise man (or more likely, a woman) once said, "The function of parents in a family is to prepare their children so well they never need them again once they leave home, but who will *want* to return often."

My years of working with kids and families have demonstrated that most of us do a pretty good job providing these skills and instilling the underlying values. As parents, we can all use a refresher (reminder) opportunity or at least a check list (like this book) so we can review how well we are doing. I call that being a *Thoughtful Parent*. In an early incarnation of this book, I considered that as the title – The Thoughtful Parent. The emphasis changed. The title changed. The importance of preparing children to cherish and contribute to their democracy did not change.

* * * * *

VALUE PAIR TWENTY-FIVE:
Cause and effect
rather than
correlation

ILLUSTRATION:

Human folks choose to 'file' their observations about the world in two main ways: *Cause and Effect* (there is proof that X caused Y) and *Correlation* (since X is present with Y, one of them caused the other or one of them explains something about it, or the two should not become separated.)

An Illustrative Caution: A study from the 1950s found that men who flew first class died from heart attacks more frequently than men who flew business. It demonstrates the basic fallacy of basing conclusions on correlation – assuming cause and effect where none is really there: [Our Deep Minds do that all the time.] What age group of men most frequently flies first class – young men early in their careers or old men who can afford to fly first class? Old men, of course. Which group is more prone to heart attacks? Old men, of course. Where they sat had nothing to do with it. Lesson learned! Be cautious of unsupported correlation.

Back to the Illustration: 1963, mid-south, USA. One summer, as a graduate student, I worked as an 'on site' family counselor in a poor area of Nashville – 99% black people. I will not forget the experiences and valuable lessons I learned. [The un-wisdom of having a white man in such a position deserves more discussion than will happen!]

"Who are you?"

A question from the spokesperson for a small group of five-year-olds.

"I'm Tom."

"You're white."

"Yes, I am."

"This place is for *black* folks."

"Why is that?"

"Just how it is."

"I like to come and talk with families here so I can get to know you."

Misunderstanding, the boy pointed to each of his friends in order, telling me their names.

"Those are great names, guys. Good to meet you."

Looks of puzzlement passed among them. A few pulled back a half step or so.

"We ain't s'posed to talk with no white men."

"Do you know why?"

The lot of them raised their skinny shoulders as if choreographed. I took a seat on the ground and leaned back against a bench.

"I suppose you better leave then."

Perhaps it had been unfair to engage their Deep Minds in that way – essentially telling them, 'NO', so they would remain. (I'm sure we've all heard the inexact term, 'Reverse Psychology'. Hmm. That Deep Mind stuff is making more and more sense.)

They gathered around, sitting cross-legged and looking me over. I removed a colorful picture book from my briefcase – illustrations of fruit and vegetables. Most of them had never seen 'raw veggies' – government commodities came mushed inside cans – so I moved on from having them name them to talking about the colors and shapes.

The head honcho of the group had an unrelated question. (Of course, he did – he was five!)

"Why are white people bad to black people?"

"Like what kinds of bad?"

Again, the wave of shrugs and blank looks.

"I'm a white man. What bad things have I done to you?"

"Nothin', *so far.*"

"You believe I'm going to do something bad to you?"

"I suppose so – you're a white man."

"Let me put it another way. What have you seen from me so far that makes you believe I'll do something bad."

"Easy. You're white."

It seemed like a slam/dunk to Jasper. His comrades agreed with determined nods.

White men are bad to black kids. I was white. I had not hurt them, but I was white. I had showed them the book and we had fun and lots of laughs at the silly things I said about it, but I was white. They didn't know why I'd want to hurt them, but, then, I was a white man so, of course, I would hurt them. Correlation!

"What about the white kids you play with? Do they want to hurt you?"

"Never played with no white kid. Like I said, this place is for black folks."

Facts, based on observable cause and effect, played no role in their beliefs about this white man. Since white men and kids were not parts of their lives, their beliefs had not been acquired from honest to goodness, black to white, relationships. Those beliefs were so deeply engrained in the community that even proof through a happy time together had no influence on their belief about the matter.

I'm not confronting the fact that the adults in their lives had a history of terrible experiences at the hands of white people. I am demonstrating that once 'lore' takes hold, 'demonstrable new facts' have little power, and if they are to come to have power, the offsetting experiences must come in regular, powerful waves. Remember how the Deep Mind builds new directives – *frequency, recency, emotional power, demonstration rather than words (through in an image for good measure)*.

I engaged the help of the youth directors of the nearby Unitarian and Lutheran churches (white) and the pastor of the local Baptist Church (black), explained my concept, and soon had a dozen, mixed race, play groups going. A month later, I was offered lemonade or cookies when I walked through that neighborhood – even by those grandmothers with the waggly fingers who had initially drawn their 'babies' close to them as I passed. I must point out, cookies for white man #1 did not translate into cookies for white men #2 or #3 . . .

Three things linger in that 60-year-old memory:

During that summer, my personal safety was threatened by both black and white gangs in the area because of what I was doing. They objected to my meddling with the lore, which was the basis of their belief systems and power. Hating each other was the balance they counted on. *Different* was to be feared because it couldn't be guaranteed to be safe – in fact, life proved it to be otherwise.

My faculty advisor called me in and said I must cease and desist immediately. My activity made it appear that the college condoned treating black people as equals to white and that it was in favor of (wait for it!) *integration*. [UGH!!! Some part of me is still embarrassed my final degree came from that school.]

The police verified that the program reduced tensions, crimes between black and white youngsters over a six square block area diminished, and the program continued on its own for years after I was long gone (gone from Nashville, you understand). Ignorance (paucity of facts based in experiences) allows and fosters prejudice and mistrust. Fact-based information fosters understanding (a fund of truths about something), tolerance if not acceptance, and cooperation.

CONCLUSION:

People that accept correlation rather than substantiated cause and effect, keep themselves dangerously ignorant. It is the basis for superstition – beliefs based in correlation. Increased fund of knowledge, knowing how things really work, and inquisitive minds, provide the solution.

Societies cannot become healthy and move forward when their people are dependent on correlation (and the lore it sets in motion) as the basis of knowledge and solutions. Dependence on substantiated cause and effect breeds a society based on facts. Without facts, society wilts because so many dangerous mistakes are made and so many opportunities are missed.

* * * * *

VALUE PAIR TWENTY-SIX:
Equitable distribution of wealth
rather than
Greed

ILLUSTRATION:

For three generations, the Wilcox family had owned thousands of acres of corn and bean growing land in the mid-west. It was some of the finest in the world. When the great grandfather – the founder of Wilcox Agri Enterprises – died, it was passed on to his son who came to be recognized as a benevolent employer – good working conditions, good hourly wage for laborers, promotion through the ranks, and top-level contracts for management. The Enterprise was professionally managed and became quite lucrative for the owner and provided security for the employees.

Upon their father's death, two sons took over. Jake was the kind who had found ways to always get the extra piece of pie or claim the best foal as his own. He was a tunnel-vision-capitalist* through and through and wanted to tighten the operation's belt, dismiss 25% of the employees, cut back on 'expensive' crop rotation and fertilization, and bring in automated machines to replace labor. He figured he could double output in two years, meaning he could double his personal income at the expense of the workers and the soil. [*life viewed according to one bottom line – maximize profit regardless of its effects on society or people.]

David, the other brother, figured with the family fortune at a staggering level, and since the families of most of the workers went back three generations with them, it was time to offer the workers non-transferable shares, with shareholders put in a position of offering guidance in how the organization would be run.

Jake opposed all of his brother's radical ideas. The Wilcox family had built the organization, had paid its employees fairly, and he had heard little dissatisfaction among the workers. He liked expensive toys – cars, boats, plains, vacations, and blonds with a

141

proclivity for expensive baubles. The previous two generations had set him up for a life of ease.

David offered to buy out his brother's share so he could proceed with his 'distribute the wealth' plan. In the end, they divided ownership fifty/fifty – it became two, side-by-side enterprises. Jake trimmed staff, increased production with automation, and his income increased pretty much according to his plan. With fewer workers, those who remained with him were pushed into longer days. Their checks did grow, and had been fairly based.

David's workers chose to take less out of the business so they could purchase additional tractors and trucks and bring a railhead right onto their land. An adjoining acreage became available and they purchased it. Over two growing seasons they brought the over-worked new land up to near par with the old land.

Five years later, Jake's land had been over-cropped. With lower yield, employees had to be let go. Still, Jake became wealthy beyond his dreams. He purchased a huge yacht and built a new, luxurious mansion.

During those same five years, David had doubled the size of his holdings while thoughtfully maintaining the quality of the soil. With two hundred employees, he established an elementary school and a medical clinic. He initiated a plan by which the workers could opt to build their own homes. Early on, they had begun a co-op that grew to provide, at discounts, most any item a family might need. There was also a small, depositor-owned, bank. The employees – at their suggestion – began a hot-house-based vegetable business they operated during the cold months. They were earning nearly twice that of Jake's mostly temporary staff.

At that point, David proposed the workers form a modest civil organization to govern itself within the laws of the state. That provided several tax advantages for them. The village of Wilcox was born.

James was one of the wealthiest men in the state, operating with overworked, seasonal, workers at local wages. David figured he (himself) had ten times what any man needed to live out his on, plus, due to his efforts, he had a happy, healthy, crew, that loved each other, him, and his family. James' Will left everything to his son who immediately bought a second yacht. David's took adequate care of his family and included several charitable features. One, left the farm to his help with several provisos to assure it could not be subdivided, sold, or squandered. Governmental and private groups regularly visited to study what David had achieved.

Such a story never stops, but enough said to contrast self-centered greed with the more equitable distribution of wealth – not as charity or the dole, but an efficient, unselfish plan. I think of it as, *Altruistic Capitalism* or as *Distributive Capitalism*, designed to be mutually beneficial, compassionate, and fair – those who do the work reap the benefits. (The knowledgeable reader will understand that is not really socialism.)

DISCUSSION:

The essential focus here addresses income inequality – a situation that kills societies and has the potential of terminating a civilized, comfortable Human species. It is already a well-established, pernicious condition in most western countries. The essential question becomes, should wealth be consolidated among a few folks (capitalism, as currently conceived, approves of that with no concern for long-term effects on people) or be more equitably distributed among all cooperating citizens (compassionate or distributive capitalism, democratic socialism, human dignity, and altruism suggest this is the approach that can save humanity.) Greedy folks, of course, aren't concerned with either the current condition of humanity in general or its future state.

A secondary question surfaces: If I earned it, shouldn't I be allowed to keep it rather than sharing it with those who are too unskilled or less lucky to do like I did? It characterizes the one asking the question as selfish and unconcerned about whether mankind continues or dies off. "Once I'm gone, who cares?"

Long, long ago, I left the church in which I was raised, but my value system continues to be quite compatible with the positive approach it took to society in general. It taught that those who have been able to be financially successful have the grand opportunity – the privilege – to help those who have little or are in financial distress. THAT, will go a long way toward saving humanity – replacing greed with altruism. The choice becomes between the overriding importance of people – humanity – or the importance of personal comfort, stuff and power. It has to be something deeper, more expansive, and more substantial than the benevolent overlord.

When we get to the place it warms our hearts more to provide a meal for a needy person than it does to gorge oneself at a fancy restaurant, we will know we are on the right track to *Saving Humanity through lives based in Positive Social Values.*

* * * * *

A Few More Pairs

Following, are several more pairs of Positive vs Negative values. Most of them have been approached in a variety of ways earlier in this section. It might be instructive to add an illustration to each of them from *your* life, and then discuss it and consider its implementation and long term effect on humanity, its comfort, and its survival.

Whenever one sets himself up as one who has the answers, (authors of a variety of bents), he runs the risk of becoming the very sort of know-it-all I have been railing against. Consider the possibility that there can be 'benevolent know-it-alls' as well as 'malevolent know-it-alls' Carefully consider the facts. In the end, of course, the call belongs to the reader. (smile)

TWENTY- SEVEN:
Trust facts and expertise
rather than
Lore or opinion

TWENTY-EIGHT:
Law-abiding behavior
rather than
law slipping behavior

TWENTY-NINE:
Earning what you need and want
rather than
merely taking it

THIRTY:
Planning ahead
rather than
Monday morning quarter-backing

THIRTY-ONE:
Health and fitness awareness
rather than
health unawareness

THIRTY-TWO:
Analytic (informed) participation
rather than
heedless (uninformed) participation

THIRTY-THREE:
Purposefully organized living style
rather than
chaotic/ haphazard living style

SECTION THREE
So What?

Here's an Idea. Instead of 'discussing' or arguing politics based within the typically, intransigent, confrontational, progressive vs conservative format, how about casting governing in terms of what is necessary for the continued, comfortable, existence of the Human Species. To that end, sit down together and begin by evaluating just one pair of Social Values (one positive and one negative) and stating what they can both agree on relative to it. Write that down and expand it into action plans. Then the next and the next. In the end there will be a list of at least 26 essential elements for human survival. There will, necessarily, emerge a consensus that saving humanity must become the overwhelming activity for all of us. One would think that would provide an excellent – non-political – starting place. That could only be the case, of course, among men who can set greed and prior animosities aside for the good of humankind, and who can agree that all people deserve the dignity that is theirs merely because they are human beings. (Some will never agree *that* is true, however.)

My informal research suggests that even with the most politically diverse folks (though sane), over 95 percent will agree that pursuing the positive value will bring the best result for our citizens – methods and financial considerations may vary. Since when have 95% of Americans agreed on anything? I used the approach successfully for 40 years in my clinical psychology practice with Teens and Families that found themselves wallowed down in intractable disagreement and turmoil. Don't discount the similarities with governing.

After finding value after value that can be agreed upon, take the next step and make plans about how the positive value can be 'activated', implemented, achieved, and preserved – not a conservative or progressive solution – a solution based on those positive values that make sense in a non-defensive, altruistic world.

Surely, that can move long-term, need-based, legislating forward in a manner that has some better chance of solving problems and helping needy people, rather than defensively maintaining a position that is often illogically counterproductive or irrelevant to the major problem at hand – the survival of humanity. Here is a sequence for us to consider. First, establish the approach within each family. (Joy and comfort are guaranteed to blossom, there.) Expand it to neighborhood and local government. Move on to larger and larger jurisdictions. Naysayers need to list well-founded objections – fact based and logical. What if it is found to only work up the line as far as neighborhoods or small towns? Isn't that where humans live and establish comfortable, productive, happy lives – the kind that save humanity? Maybe it needs to go no further.

I do believe I read somewhere that the essence of living well together is to treat others the way we need to be treated – make sure others have what they need the way I make sure I have what I need. All major religions contain that requirement for the good life. It would seem major religions have very little influence on the way the people of the world operate. So sad, isn't it?

It means setting aside 'me' for 'us' where 'us' means ALL of us. We still don't seem very close to being willing to do that, do we?

So much to think about and so little time to respond. I suspect that until a generation is raised in the tradition of Positive Social Values, the aspirations I envision may not come to fruition. I do hope the traditional dark side of human beings does not ultimately preclude the vision.

Along the way, procedures must be discovered and implemented to handle the ever-present, malevolent greedy and forever evil among us. Nothing says we must allow them to either negatively affect us or destroy us. The good guys, the benevolent guys, the altruistic and the positive, thoughtful guys must take charge.

Read voraciously. Live thoughtfully. Vote intelligently. And always be kind.

Please forgive the naivete of the presentation.
Naivete often represents simplicity.
The human species has been wallowing in confusing complexity
for most of its existence.
Let's give simplicity a go by raising new generations of
Human Beings that accept and practice
Positive Social Values
and program the negative ones into oblivion.

– Tom Gnagey

Appendix: The Value Pairs

ONE:
Logical problem-solving techniques.
rather than
physical aggression

TWO:
Accepting others as they are
rather than
trying to change them

THREE:
Universal dignity among men
rather than
Self-righteous bigotry

FOUR:
Cooperative approach to living
rather than
an unbridled competitive approach to living.

FIVE:
Ability to delay gratification
rather than
the need for immediate gratification.

SIX:
A save and pay as you go approach,
rather than
irresponsible spend & credit approach.

SEVEN:
Helpful
rather than
hurtful (including ignoring)

EIGHT:
Taking responsibility
rather than
blaming

NINE:
Reverence and respect for life
rather than
disregard for life

TEN:
Altruism
rather than
selfishness

ELEVEN:
Accurately informed decision making
rather than
uninformed or lore-base decision making

TWELVE:
Being known by ones good reputation
rather than
trying to be known as a somebody at any cost

THIRTEEN:
Kind-hearted
rather than
inconsiderate or otherwise hurtful

FOURTEEN:
Try to understand others who are different
rather than
Ignore, exclude, or hurt them.

FIFTEEN:
Seek to understand Intentions
rather than
Assuming you understand a person's motivation

SIXTEEN:
Fair treatment and honesty
rather than
deceit and dishonesty

SEVENTEEN:
Positive value-based openness
rather than
belief in mindless absolute right and wrong

EIGHTEEN:
Finding purpose and happiness through integrity
rather than
seeking it through stuff, status, or power

NINETEEN:
Youngsters having adult confidantes
rather than
only having peer confidantes

TWENTY:
Reconciliation
rather than
Revenge

TWENTY-ONE:
Knowing one is a worthy being
rather than
having to keep trying to prove one is a worthy being.

TWENTY-TWO:
A user of precise language
rather than
imprecise Language

TWENTY-THREE:
Cherishing individual freedom
of belief and behavior
rather than
Assuming others must believe
and act like you.

TWENTY-FOUR:
Democratic approach
rather than
Dictatorial, strong-arm approach

TWENTY-FIVE:
Cause and effect filer
rather than
a correlation filer

TWENTY- SIX:
Equitable distribution of wealth
rather than
Greed

TWENTY- SEVEN:
Trust facts and expertise
rather than
Lore or opinion

TWENTY-EIGHT:
Peer plus family/adult social orientation
rather than
peer-only social orientation

TWENTY-NINE:
Law-abiding behavior
rather than
law slipping behavior

THIRTY:
Earning what you need and want
rather than
merely taking it

THIRTY-ONE:
Planning ahead
rather than
Monday morning quarter-backing

THIRTY-TWO:
Health and fitness awareness
rather than
health unawareness

THIRTY-THREE:
Analytic (informed) participation
rather than
heedless (uninformed) participation

THIRTY-FOUR:
Purposefully organized living style
rather than
chaotic/ haphazard living style